T0248533

Pup-Approved
DOG TREAT
RECIPES

Homemade Goodies from
Paddington's Pantry

CAYLA GALLAGHER,
CERTIFIED PET NUTRITION COACH

Skyhorse Publishing

Skyhorse Publishing books may be purchased in bulk at special discounts for sales promotion, corporate gifts, fund-raising, or educational purposes. Special editions can also be created to specifications. For details, contact the Special Sales Department, Skyhorse Publishing, 307 West 36th Street, 11th Floor, New York, NY 10018 or info@skyhorsepublishing.com.

Skyhorse® and Skyhorse Publishing® are registered trademarks of Skyhorse Publishing, Inc.®, a Delaware corporation.

Visit our website at www.skyhorsepublishing.com.

10 9 8 7 6 5 4 3

Library of Congress Cataloging-in-Publication Data

Names: Gallagher, Cayla, author.
Title: Pup-approved dog treat recipes: homemade goodies from Paddington's pantry / Cayla Gallagher, certified pet nutrition coach.
Description: New York, NY: Skyhorse Publishing, [2021] | Includes index. |
Identifiers: LCCN 2020046949 (print) | LCCN 2020046950 (ebook) | ISBN 9781510759558 (hardback) | ISBN 9781510759565 (ebook)
Subjects: LCSH: Dogs—Food—Recipes. | Dogs—Nutrition.
Classification: LCC SF427.4 .G345 2021 (print) | LCC SF427.4 (ebook) | DDC 636.7/083—dc23
LC record available at https://lccn.loc.gov/2020046949
LC ebook record available at https://lccn.loc.gov/2020046950

Cover design by Daniel Brount
Cover photos by Cayla Gallagher
Graphic illustrations by @cockatoo_design

Print ISBN: 978-1-5107-5955-8
Ebook ISBN: 978-1-5107-5956-5

Printed in China

CONTENTS

INTRODUCTION

Hello and welcome to my *fourth* (pinches self) cookbook! I am so incredibly excited that this time I get to share my dogs and their favorite treat recipes with you. This idea has been brewing in my mind for years and I truly believe this is my best work thus far.

I'd like to introduce you to my "co-authors," Paddington and Treacle, my two Pomeranians. Paddington is four years old and is a total foodie—he's been begging for table scraps since I brought him home. Treacle is two years old, fully grown at three pounds, and prances like a little pony whenever her food bowl is filled. I've always loved for Paddington and Treacle to experience a variety of flavors and textures. It's the most adorable thing to see their expressions when they taste something new, especially something that they fall in love with immediately. I hope that when making these recipes, you'll have these heartwarming moments with your pup too!

These recipes are meant to be primarily treats and snacks for your dog, not meal replacements. Every dog's diet and needs are different, and I know that as a loving, responsible pet owner, you know exactly what your dog should be eating on a daily basis. These recipes are just fun little additions to make when they deserve something special. I have included recipes that are more savory than sweet, such as my Steak & Sweet Potato Stew (page 197) or Nana's Risotto (page 205), but I still serve these in small, snack-sized portions to my pups and freeze the rest. So don't worry about making a big batch—the freezer is your friend! You'll save time and money and these treats will last a long time when frozen. Simply defrost a small portion in the fridge overnight and surprise your dog the next day!

It is also very important to me that you feel comfortable and confident making these recipes for your precious fur baby. Paddington and Treacle are like my children, and when following recipes, I want to feel secure in knowing that the ingredients are safe and healthy for

them. So before writing this book, I got my certification as a pet nutrition coach. I have created a Food Safety Guide (page 3) that outlines foods that are safe and dangerous for dogs, as well as explaining why. I want to empower you to understand what you're putting into their system and know how each ingredient is benefitting your beloved pet.

However, every dog is unique in their sensitivities and dietary needs. I highly recommend checking with your vet before introducing any new foods, ingredients, or treats into your dog's diet to be certain that your dog stays healthy—they're certain to love all these recipes, but their health is always the top priority.

FOOD SAFETY GUIDE

As much as your pup may beg for a bite of your dinner, it's incredibly important to know which ingredients are safe for them to consume. When making treats for your dog, refer to this list to make sure that your fur baby stays healthy and safe! However, every dog has different needs and sensitivities, so double-check with your vet before making any homemade treats or introducing a new food into their diet.

No-No Foods

ALCOHOL—Alcohol is very toxic to dogs, even in small amounts and when incorporated in food products. Never give your dogs anything cooked with alcohol. It can cause vomiting, diarrhea, decreased coordination, central nervous system depression, tremors, difficulty breathing, coma, and sometimes death.

AVOCADO—The seed, skin, and leaves of avocados contain a toxin called persin, which can cause vomiting and diarrhea in dogs. The flesh doesn't contain as much persin, but is still unsafe for dogs. Sadly, no avocado toast for your pup!

BLUE CHEESE—The fungus used to produce these cheeses produces a substance called roquefortine C. Dogs can be sensitive to this fungus and it can cause vomiting, diarrhea, muscle tremors, and seizures.

BUTTER AND MARGARINE—Due to the high fat content, these are best avoided. When a dog consumes too much fat, the pancreas can become inflamed, also known as pancreatitis. Pancreatitis needs to be treated in hospital, so stick with healthier alternatives when cooking, like coconut oil.

CHOCOLATE—Just like caffeine, chocolate contains methylxanthines. It also contains theobromine, a chemical that is poisonous to dogs. The darker and more bitter the chocolate, the higher the levels of theobromine, therefore making dark and milk chocolate much more toxic than white chocolate (though this still contains high quantities of fat, which can cause pancreatitis).

CINNAMON—Generally not harmful to dogs in small quantities. It takes more than 1 teaspoon of cinnamon to cause an issue, however this may vary depending on the size of the dog, especially if they are tiny. Large cinnamon overdoses can cause diarrhea, vomiting, changes in heart rate, low blood sugar, and liver disease. I tend to stay away from cinnamon because my dogs are so small, and any benefit they could get from cinnamon is negligible. If you're looking for a festive touch to add to cookies, ginger is a much better alternative.

COFFEE, CAFFEINE, AND SODAS—These contain substances called methylxanthines, which can cause vomiting, diarrhea, panting, excessive thirst and urination, hyperactivity, abnormal heart rhythm, seizures, and sometimes death.

FRUIT PITS AND SEEDS—Seeds from pears and apples, and pits from mangoes, cherries, peaches, and plums contain cyanide. Cyanide disrupts cellular transport, meaning that blood cells become unable to get enough oxygen. It's best to discard the seeds and pits completely and just give your pup the fruity flesh to snack on.

GARLIC—This is sometimes a controversial ingredient. Garlic belongs to the allium family, which also includes onions, leeks, and chives. All plants in this family contain a substance which can damage red blood cells and can cause life-threatening anemia. After consulting with Paddington's vet, it seems that the quantity of garlic deemed harmful varies for each dog, so I recommend avoiding it completely.

GRAPES, RAISINS, AND CURRANTS—These have been proven to be very toxic to dogs and can cause kidney failure, sometimes delayed by up to three days. Check for signs of decreased urination or increased thirst and always call your vet if your dog eats any amount.

HOT DOGS—If your pup sneakily steals a hot dog from your plate (looking at you, Paddington), it's not worth a trip to the emergency room; however hot dogs do contain ingredients that aren't the best for dogs. They can contain monosodium glutamate (MSG), sodium nitrate, which has been linked to cancer, artificial sweeteners, and seasonings. Many of these seasonings contain onion and garlic powder, which are toxic to dogs. Hot dogs are also very high in salt, so top off your dog's water bowl if they sneak one.

MACADAMIA NUTS—These nuts can cause sluggishness and wobbly walking, vomiting, weakness, tremors, and hyperthermia (increase in body temperature).

MOLDY FOOD—These can contain a variety of toxins. One particular toxin commonly found on moldy bread, nuts, and dairy products can cause your pup to develop muscle tremors and seizures.

TREACLE TIP: *Keep your compost bin in an area that is inaccessible to your dog!*

MUSHROOMS—These can be very toxic for dogs. While not every single species of mushroom is considered toxic, those that are toxic can have very serious side effects—even death—so they are best to be avoided completely.

NUTMEG—Contains the toxin myristicin, which can cause hallucinations, increased heart rate, high blood pressure, dry mouth, disorientation, abdominal pain, and sometimes seizures. These symptoms generally occur when large quantities are consumed, but it's best to avoid the spice completely.

ONIONS, LEEKS, AND CHIVES—These can cause your dog's red blood cells to rupture, as well as cause vomiting, diarrhea, stomach pain, and nausea.

RAW BREAD DOUGH—Uncooked yeast can rise in the stomach and cause gas to accumulate. This can cause pain for your poor pup, and even worse, the bloated stomach can twist and become life-threatening. Yeast also produces ethanol as a by-product, which can cause the same symptoms as if they directly consumed alcohol.

 RAW POTATO—Dogs should never be fed raw potatoes. Raw potatoes contain solanine, a compound that is toxic to some dogs. Cooking the potato reduces the levels of solanine, so if you do feed your dog potato, it should be baked or boiled.

RHUBARB—Rhubarb leaves contain soluble oxalate crystals, which can cause poisoning in dogs. Symptoms include drooling, vomiting, diarrhea, lethargy, tremors, bloody urine, weakness, and sometimes acute renal failure.

SWORDFISH—Fish are a fabulous source of omega-3 fatty acids. However, longer-lived fish species like swordfish should be avoided. It can contain heavy metals like mercury, which can build up in the system over time and lead to heavy metal toxicity. Stick with short-lived fish like salmon, herring, whitefish, Arctic char, and flounder.

 XYLITOL—This is an artificial sweetener and is used as a sugar replacement. It is very poisonous to dogs and can cause their blood sugar levels to dangerously drop, sometimes causing liver failure.

Yes-Yes Foods

APPLES—A wonderful source of vitamin A, C, and fiber. Just be sure to remove the core and seeds, as they can contain traces of cyanide.

BANANA—Low calorie and high in potassium, vitamins, biotin, fiber, and copper. They do have a high sugar content, so only use bananas as a treat.

BEEF—I don't have to tell you that no dog will turn down a hearty steak! Beef is high in vitamin B_{12}, B_3, B_6, protein, iron, zinc, and selenium. Beef is actually a common food allergy for dogs, so if your dog is showing signs of an allergy, beef may be a culprit.

BLUEBERRIES—Rich in antioxidants and phytochemicals, which help to prevent cell damage in your pup. They are also full of fiber and are an easy treat to use for training. The only risk is their size, as they are a potential choking hazard, especially if frozen. I like to select the biggest blueberries and keep an eye on Paddington and Treacle as they snack.

TREACLE TIP: *Paddington taught me that blueberries don't come as singles, so if mummy or daddy gives you one, they have more somewhere. Don't settle for just one blueberry!*

CANTALOUPE—Low in calories, packed with nutrients, and is a great source of fiber and water. It is high in sugar, so only give this as a treat.

CARROTS—Low calorie and very high in fiber and beta-carotene, which produces vitamin A. Munching on carrots are also a great way to help keep your dog's teeth clean. I like to give carrots a thorough wash but keep the skin on, as it contains lots of nutrients. Sometimes my pups get a large carrot to play with over a few days, or mini carrots that they can enjoy in an afternoon.

CELERY—A magical breath freshener! Celery also contains vitamins A, B, and C, and helps promote a healthy heart. The long fibers can sometimes be overwhelming to dogs, so I cut celery into diagonal 1-inch pieces before giving it as a snack.

CHIA SEEDS—Rich in omega-3 fatty acids, chia seeds are a great alternative for dogs who are sensitive to fish and fish oil. They are also a great source of fiber, manganese, copper, and zinc.

CHICKEN—Of course chicken is safe! It is a good source of protein and can be used as a special treat. Be sure to remove the bone before serving, as cooked chicken bones can splinter easily and make your pup choke or cause a gastrointestinal puncture. Chicken is also a common allergen for dogs, so take note if your dog is showing signs of allergies.

COCONUT—Coconut meat is high in lauric acid, which helps fight influenza, yeast infections, ringworm, and giardia, and can also help speed the healing of cuts and hot spots and potentially soothe inflamed joints from arthritis. Make sure to remove the shell and only provide the meat as a snack. Coconut oil is also a wonderful ingredient to promote a healthy coat, as well as topically for hot spots or itchy, dry skin. Be sure to use the highest quality unrefined coconut oil, a.k.a. virgin coconut oil or cold-pressed coconut oil.

 CRANBERRIES—These can be eaten by your dog fresh or dried, as long as they are natural and unsweetened. They are quite tart, so this might be a controversial flavor! Paddington happily ate one, while Treacle took one lick and walked away in disgust.

CUCUMBER—A great treat for your dog, as they contain vitamins B_1, C, K, potassium, copper, magnesium, and biotin. They are also very low in fat and carbohydrates, so are a wonderful option for overweight pups. Paddington likes to take a slice and eat just the centers of cucumbers, leaving the outer ring with skin completely intact. So hilarious!

EGGS—High in protein and contain many fatty acids and essential amino acids. Raw eggs may cause biotin deficiency due to the enzyme avidin, which prevents the absorption of biotin, which supports healthy metabolism, skin, digestion, and cells. Cooking the egg eliminates this risk, which is why I usually cook the doggies' eggs before serving. Unless an egg falls on the ground while baking . . . in those cases, I thank Paddington for being my clean-up crew!

GELATIN—A wonderful ingredient to use in dog treats, gelatin contains amino acids that are beneficial for your dog's skin, hair, and joint health. Do *not* use Jell-O or any sugary jelly packets. These can contain flavorings and artificial sweeteners, which can be toxic. The only gelatin that you should be using is plain, powdered gelatin that is unflavored and unsweetened.

GINGER—A wonderful ingredient that helps reduce nausea and has also been used in treatment of cardiovascular disorders. Does your pup get carsick? Incorporate some fresh or ground ginger in your next batch of cookies and give them one before your next car ride!

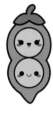

GREEN BEANS & PEAS—A fabulous source of fiber and low in calories. Paddington is a huge fan of sugar snap peas. I've used them as potty-training treats for both dogs and they are always snatched out of my hand and promptly eaten.

HONEY—Local honey contains the local pollen that will affect your pup, and helps their body create antibodies. A lick of honey is also great to soothe a sore throat, or to help catch any pieces of fluff that are tickling your dog's throat. However, be careful giving raw honey to puppies and dogs with compromised immune systems, as it may contain botulism spores. Honey is also very high in sugar, so only give your dog a lick or two at a time. Honey is also packed with nutrients such as vitamin A, C, B, D, E, and K, potassium, calcium, magnesium, and copper. It can also be used topically for burns and superficial cuts.

Peaches—A wonderful source of fiber and vitamin A. Be sure to remove the pit before giving them to your pup, as the pit contains cyanide. They are great eaten fresh or frozen, but avoid canned peaches as they usually contain lots of sugary syrup.

Pineapple—Contains an enzyme called bromelain, which makes it easier for dogs to absorb proteins. It is also packed full of vitamins, minerals, and fiber—just be sure to remove the outer peel and spiky crown before serving.

 Pork—Pork is less likely to cause allergic reactions in some dogs, compared to beef and chicken. It is a highly digestible protein and is packed with amino acids.

Pumpkin—A wonderful fiber-rich vegetable, which contains vitamin A, C, and E, potassium, and iron. Pumpkin is a wonderful digestive aid, particularly if your pup is suffering from constipation or diarrhea (yes, both!). The soluble fiber in pumpkin adds bulk to the stool by absorbing water, and the fermentation of the fiber produces fatty acids, which provide energy to cells, stimulate water and sodium absorption in the intestines, and lower the pH level of the large intestines. When purchasing pumpkin, I recommend plain, canned pumpkin. *Not* pumpkin pie filling, which is typically sweetened! And because upset tummies are, unfortunately, unpredictable, I spoon the pumpkin into an ice cube tray and keep it in the freezer. Then just pop a cube of frozen pumpkin into their food bowl whenever they have an upset tummy.

Quinoa—A healthy alternative to corn, wheat, and soy, and it is frequently included in some high quality dry dog foods. I use quinoa flour in baked goods for my pups, but if you are looking to use it as a grain, I recommend washing it first. This is because the quinoa plant contains a chemical called saponin, which protects itself from insects. It is suggested that this may cause stomach irritation in dogs, but washing the quinoa before cooking should remove most of it.

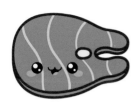

Salmon—A fabulous source of omega-3 fatty acids, an essential "good" type of fat which keeps your pup's coat looking shiny and healthy, as well as helps the immune system and decreases inflammation. It is also a great source of protein. Salmon oil is additionally rich in omega-6 fatty acids and supports heart health and cognitive function. It also helps to reduce itchy, flaky skin.

Sardines—Like all fish, sardines contain food fats and amino acids. Sardines are extra beneficial because they have soft, digestible bones that give your dog extra calcium. Paddington's breeder suggested I place a canned sardine or two in his food bowl every so often as a treat, but to be completely honest,  the fear of a sardine being hidden under my couch has deterred me all these years! My living room feels much safer when the sardines are baked into cookies instead! When purchasing sardines, I try to find sardines packed in water and without any extra seasonings.

Spirulina—Contains several phytonutrients that strengthen the immune system, improve gastrointestinal health, and help allergies. This is a great ingredient to add a pinch to cookies, providing health benefits as well as a beautiful color! Blue, and most common, blue-green spirulina are used in this book as natural coloring agents!

Strawberries—Strawberries contain an enzyme that can help whiten your pup's (and your!) teeth, as well as lots of fiber and vitamin C.

Sweet Potato—The health benefits of sweet potato are the same for dogs are they are for you! They are a wonderful source of fiber, which aids in digestion. They are also low in fat and rich in vitamin A, C, B_6, calcium, potassium, and iron. Sweet potato treats were the first treat I bought for Paddington as a puppy, so it holds a special place in my heart.

TURKEY—Found in many commercial dog foods and contains nutrients such as riboflavin, protein, and phosphorous. However, before serving to your dog, be sure to remove any excess fat, skin, bones, and seasonings cooked alongside it. I know your pup may tell you otherwise, but a Thanksgiving turkey with all the trimmings isn't for them!

 WATERMELON—A wonderful way to keep your fur baby hydrated, as it contains 92 percent water! It is also packed full of vitamins A, B_6, and C. Make sure to remove the rind and seeds first, as they can sometimes cause intestinal blockage.

WHEAT & GRAINS—Contrary to the guilt-inducing grain-free dog food fad, it is actually okay for dogs to have grains. Wheat and corn are great sources of protein, essential fatty acids, and fiber. Some dogs may be allergic to wheat, but make sure to confirm the allergy with your vet and ask for recommendations if deciding to alter your dog's diet.

Sometimes Foods

CHEESE—A great, and delicious, treat to give dogs. It can be quite high in fat, so aim for lower-fat cheeses such as cottage cheese or mozzarella. It can be chopped into very tiny pieces and used as quick and easy training treats!

HAM—Okay as a treat, but as it is high in sodium and fat, shouldn't be given very often.

PEANUTS—Full of good fats and proteins. Make sure to only give them unsalted peanuts and in moderation, as the consumption of too much fat can lead to pancreatitis.

POPCORN—Contains riboflavin and thiamine, which promote digestion and eye health. Serve your pup unsalted, unbuttered, air-popped popcorn and be sure to pop the kernels fully before giving them to your dog. Unpopped kernels can be a choking hazard. The speed at which Paddington flies onto the couch when he sees me eating popcorn is a sight that I wish you all could behold!

TUNA—Okay for dogs, and when cooked fresh, it is a great source of omega-3 fatty acids, which promote eye and heart health. When using canned tuna, only purchase tuna prepared in water, not oil, and not containing any extra flavors or spices. Tuna is a longer-lived fish species, meaning that it contains small amounts of mercury, so I recommend only giving tuna sparingly.

Use Caution Foods

BONES—Raw meat bones are the best dog bones. When cooked, bones become brittle and can splinter. Chicken, turkey, and goose bones are particularly easy to splinter. Splintered bones can cause a digestive obstruction, while smaller pieces can irritate or even puncture the stomach or intestine. Pork bones, particularly pork rib bones, are high in fat and can lead to pancreatitis if too much fat is consumed. Also be sure to dispose of a bone after 3–4 days, as bacteria can grow and cause intestinal upset. Lastly, supervise your dog when they are chewing on a bone. You need to be able to take the bone away if it starts to break or if it is getting too small. Bones should be larger than the dog's muzzle, so that there is no risk of being swallowed whole.

 BROCCOLI—Can be served cooked or raw and is high in fiber and vitamin C. Broccoli florets contain isothiocyanates, which can lead to mild to severe gastric irritation in some dogs. It's important that broccoli is given only as a small snack and be sure to monitor your dog to see how they feel. Broccoli stalks have also been known to obstruct the esophagus, especially in small dogs, so be sure to chop the broccoli into small pieces before serving.

BRUSSELS SPROUTS—Very nutritious for your dog! They contain vitamin A, C, B_1, B_6, and K. They also contain fiber and antioxidants, which help reduce inflammation and improve blood circulation. The downside is that they give your puppy gas—quite a lot of gas. Too many Brussels sprouts may cause an upset tummy, but even small amounts cause doggy toots. These are technically harmless, but it's really up to what you think your nose can handle!

 CHERRIES—The flesh of cherries is safe for dogs to eat; the problem lies within the stem, leaves, and pit. They contain cyanide, which is poisonous and potentially lethal. The pits can also cause intestinal blockage.

MILK—Dogs can have a little bit of milk—however some dogs are lactose-intolerant and don't digest it very well. I recommend giving it in minimal quantities, and when it comes across in baking, substitute it for broth or water.

 ORANGES—Packed with nutrients and fiber and low in sodium. They are also full of vitamin C, which promotes the immune system. However, oranges are moderately high in sugar and can cause an upset stomach if your dog eats too much. Peel the orange, remove any seeds, and only give your dog a little at a time. I usually stick with one clementine segment each for Paddington and Treacle.

PEANUT BUTTER—An excellent source of protein and contains vitamins B and E, niacin, and heart-healthy fats. When shopping for peanut butter, carefully check the ingredients to be sure that the peanut butter does not contain xylitol, which is very toxic to dogs. The best peanut butter for dogs is raw, unsalted, and contains only peanuts.

 RASPBERRIES—Safe for your dog to eat, but only in moderation. Raspberries are an excellent source of vitamin C, K, B-complex, fiber, and minerals such as iron, folic acid, copper, magnesium, potassium, and manganese. They also contain antioxidants, which reduce the chances of heart disease, cancer, diabetes, and arthritis. The risk of raspberries is that they contain the highest levels of natural xylitol, which is very toxic to dogs. Raspberries can be eaten, but only in moderation. I only give my dogs one or two raspberries at a time, but I recommend checking with your vet first.

Spinach—This is a controversial one! Spinach contains lots of vitamins, such as vitamin A, B, C, and K. It also contains iron, beta-carotene, and roughage, which stimulates digestion. However, spinach is very high in oxalic acid, which blocks your pup's ability to absorb calcium and can cause kidney damage. It is generally agreed upon that dogs would need to consume a large amount of spinach to cause damage, but

long-term consumption can cause stress on the kidneys, muscle weakness, irregular heart rhythms, and respiratory paralysis. If you do choose to give your dog spinach, make sure to cook it and chop it, as this is easier on your dog's system. Only feed it to your dog in sporadic, small quantities, and make sure to check with your vet before using spinach as a snack option.

Tomato—Young, green tomatoes, as well as all tomato leaves and stems contain a substance called solanine, which is harmful to dogs in large quantities. They can cause an upset tummy, loss of coordination, muscle weakness, tremors, and seizures. Red, ripe tomatoes are generally safe for dogs to eat and are suitable as an occasional snack. Just be sure to fence off any tomato plants you have in your garden.

Yogurt—When choosing yogurt, be sure to select a yogurt without any additional flavors, sugar, or artificial sweeteners. I recommend using 2% plain Greek yogurt and making sure the only ingredients listed are partly skimmed milk and bacterial culture. The active bacteria in yogurt can strengthen the digestive system with probiotics. Some dogs are sensitive to dairy, so keep an eye on your pup when first trying it.

FUNDAMENTALS

How to Fill a KONG + 5 Easy Fillings

KONGs can be filled with so many different goodies. I used to just spread some peanut butter inside and Paddington and Treacle were thrilled, but I've learned that there is actually a strategy to filling them. Want to be dog mom or dad of the year? Keep reading.

Step 1: Amuse-bouche
A delicious start to your pup's KONG adventure. Fill the tiny, top hole of the KONG with something soft or spreadable, like peanut butter, cheese, mashed banana, canned pumpkin, or baked and mashed sweet potato.

Step 2: Dessert
It may seem strange for dessert to be Step 2, but this is the next area that will be filled! Fill the first internal ⅓ of the KONG with dog treats, like crushed bones, dried liver treats, or homemade cookies.

Step 3: Entrée
Fill the remaining ⅔ with a healthier filling. Combine your dog's usual food with some mashed banana, pumpkin, or sweet potato.

Step 4: Appetizer
Entice your pup to investigate with this appetizer. Stick a treat such as a bone, liver treat, mini carrot, or any other delicious treat into the large opening of the KONG, so it's sticking right out.

At this point, give the whole treat to your dog, or place it in the freezer for 1 to 2 hours for a longer-lasting treat!

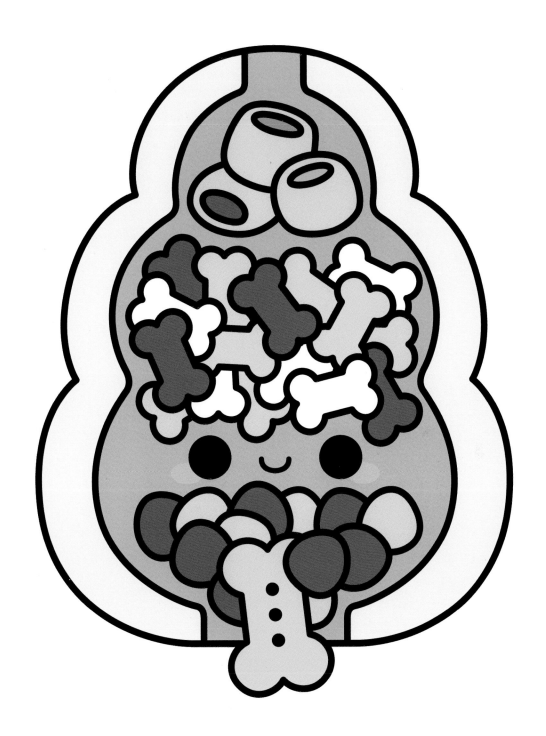

Puptella FILLING

A fun, dog-friendly twist on the popular hazelnut spread!

———————————————— MAKES ½ CUP ————————————————

¼ cup plain canned pumpkin
¼ cup natural peanut butter
1 tablespoon carob powder

1. Combine all the ingredients together in a bowl. Spoon this into the KONG.

2. Give this to your pup straight away, or place it in the freezer for about an hour before serving for a longer-lasting snack.

> **TREACLE TIP:** *Because this filling doesn't contain any chunks, this is a great option if you are nervous about choking hazards, or if your dog is missing teeth.*

5-Layer FANTASY

Packed with protein and healthy fats, this is as much a treat for your dog's taste buds as it is a healthy boost! If your dog doesn't eat kibble on a daily basis, you can substitute the kibble with dry liver treats.

──────────── QUANTITY DEPENDS ON THE SIZE OF YOUR KONG ────────────

Peanut butter
Your dog's daily kibble
Sweet potato, cooked and mashed
Canned salmon, drained and rinsed
Banana, sliced

1. Add a dollop of peanut butter into the bottom of the KONG. Then fill it ¼ of the way with kibble.

2. Mash together the sweet potato and salmon in a small bowl. Spoon it into the KONG until it is ½ full.

3. Next, add a slice of banana. To finish, combine some more peanut butter and kibble in a small bowl. Fill the KONG the rest of the way with the mixture.

4. Give this to your dog fresh, or place in the freezer for 1 to 2 hours before serving.

TREACLE TIP: *To cook the sweet potato, prick it with a fork a few times, place it on a baking sheet, and bake it whole at 425°F for 45 to 55 minutes. Short on time? Prick it with a fork, wrap it in plastic wrap, and microwave for 5 minutes!*

Breath Refresh FILLING

Every dog needs some help with their breath from time to time, and this filling is a perfect way to freshen their breath while keeping them entertained.

—————————————— MAKES ½ CUP ——————————————

½ tablespoon fresh mint leaves
1½ tablespoons fresh parsley leaves
1 banana

1. Finely chop the mint and parsley leaves. Add these to a bowl with the banana and mash with a fork until everything is well combined.

2. Spoon the filling into a KONG. Give it to your pup fresh, or freeze for 1 to 2 hours for a longer lasting snack!

Chicken Salad Sammie
FILLING

I, personally, am a huge fan of chicken salad sandwiches, so I couldn't leave out Paddington and Treacle! Chicken is a great source of protein, yogurt is very beneficial to the digestive system, and the fiber in the fruits and veggies help keep your pup regular!

———————————————— MAKES ROUGHLY 1 CUP ————————————————

½ cooked chicken breast, shredded
¼ cup finely chopped celery
¼ apple, finely chopped
2 tablespoons parsley, finely chopped
½ cup plain yogurt

1. Combine all the ingredients in a bowl.

2. Spoon the filling into a KONG. Give it to your pup fresh, or freeze for 1 to 2 hours for a longer lasting snack!

Meaty Delight FILLING

Protein is a significant part of your dog's diet and nutritional needs, so this filling is a wonderful option! We're also including carrot and pumpkin, which are high in fiber and vitamins.

———————————— MAKES ABOUT 1 CUP OF FILLING ————————————

¼ cup dry liver treats, crushed

⅓ cup cooked chicken, finely chopped

½ cup grated carrot

½ cup plain canned pumpkin

1. Combine all the ingredients together in a bowl. Spoon this into the KONG.

2. Give this to your pup straight away, or place it in the freezer for 1 to 2 hours for a longer-lasting snack.

> **TREACLE TIP:** *If your dog is sensitive to chicken, cooked ground beef or canned salmon are great alternatives!*

Treacle's TRAINING TREATS

Training treats are fundamental to every dog's life. A lot of homemade training treat recipes have you painstakingly cut out a million mini cookies, but I am far too impatient for that. Here is a cool trick to create hundreds of little treats while saving your time and your lower back!

―――――――――――――― MAKES ABOUT 4 CUPS ――――――――――――――

2 large eggs
1 banana
⅓ cup peanut butter
2½ cups quick oats

TREACLE TIP: *Add a few tablespoons of flax seeds to the batter for even higher nutritional value!*

1. Preheat the oven to 375°F.

2. Place the eggs, banana, and peanut butter in a bowl and beat with an electric mixer until combined.

3. Place the quick oats into a food processor and pulse until they resemble flour. Add the oats to the wet mixture and combine well.

4. Pour the mixture onto a large baking sheet lined with parchment paper. Use a rubber spatula to smooth the dough to ¼-inch thick.

5. Use a sharp knife to score ½-inch-thick lines over the entire sheet of dough. Bake for 15 to 20 minutes, until it's begun to brown.

6. Allow the cookie to cool completely while still on the baking sheet. Once the cookie is cool, bend the cookie to break it along the scored lines. Then break these into smaller cookies.

7. Store these cookies in the fridge for up to 1 week, or up to 3 months in the freezer.

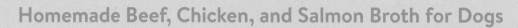

Homemade Beef, Chicken, and Salmon Broth for Dogs

Broth, or stock, is frequently used in dog food recipes. It is a wonderfully nutritious ingredient, however broth sold for humans can be dangerous as it can contain onion and garlic, which is toxic for dogs. I recommend making your own stock, so that you know exactly what it contains.

Beef BROTH

1 tablespoon liquid coconut oil
1 large carrot, roughly chopped
1 celery stalk, cut into ¼-inch slices
2½ pounds beef soup bones, with
    marrow
8 cups water

1. Set a large pot to medium heat. Add the coconut oil, carrot, and celery, and sauté until fragrant, about 3 to 5 minutes.

2. Add the beef bones and water. Increase the heat to medium-high and bring to a boil.

3. Partially cover the pot and boil for 2 hours, or until the cartilage has dissolved and the bones are stripped of their meat.

4. Remove the bones and veggies from the pot. If the beef bones still contain marrow, remove the marrow with a spoon and mix it with their kibble for a very special treat!

5. The broth should last for 5 days in the fridge, or up to 3 months in the freezer.

TREACLE TIP: *Do not take my marrow bone!*

Chicken BROTH

1 tablespoon liquid coconut oil
1 large carrot, roughly chopped
1 celery stalk, cut into ¼-inch slices
Bones of 1 whole chicken
8 cups water

1. Set a large pot to medium heat. Add the coconut oil, carrot, and celery, and sauté until fragrant, about 3 to 5 minutes.

2. Add the chicken bones and water. Increase the heat to medium-high and bring to a boil.

3. Partially cover the pot and boil for 2 hours, or until the cartilage has dissolved and the bones are stripped of their meat.

4. Pour the broth through a cheesecloth to achieve a beautiful clear broth.

5. The broth should last for 5 days in the fridge, or up to 3 months in the freezer.

Salmon BROTH

1 tablespoon liquid coconut oil
1 large carrot, roughly chopped
1 celery stalk, cut into ¼-inch slices
1 fresh salmon head
8 cups water

1. Set a large pot to medium heat. Add the coconut oil, carrot, and celery, and sauté until fragrant, about 3 to 5 minutes.

2. Add the salmon head and water. Increase the heat to medium-high and bring to a boil.

3. Partially cover the pot and boil for 2 hours, or until the salmon is very tender and falling apart.

4. Discard the salmon and pour the broth through a cheesecloth to achieve a beautiful clear broth.

5. The broth should last for 5 days in the fridge, or up to 3 months in the freezer.

TREACLE TIP: *Save yourself the hassle of making fresh broth for every recipe by making a large batch of broth and freezing it in ice cube trays! Just thaw some cubes whenever you need them.*

Classic DOG BONES

An absolute necessity and hypoallergenic! If your dog has an egg, beef, or wheat allergy, these are a great option. If they are sensitive to chicken, simply use some beef or salmon broth instead. This dough is very versatile and can be pressed into silicone molds, as well as rolled out with a rolling pin or placed into a cookie press. The possibilities are endless!

——————————— MAKES ABOUT 40 (1-INCH) TREATS ———————————

1¼ cups brown rice flour
¼ cup liquid coconut oil, plus more for the pan
⅔ cup chicken broth

TREACLE TIP: *This dough is very pale, so it's perfect for adding color to! Use some beet powder for pink dough or turmeric powder for yellow dough!*

1. Preheat oven to 325°F.

2. Combine all ingredients in a bowl. The dough should resemble playdough. If it's too dry, add an extra 1 to 2 tablespoons of chicken broth.

3. If using a silicone mold (like I did), lightly grease the mold with some extra coconut oil. Press the dough into the mold, making sure to get it into all crevices. If using a baking sheet, roll the dough out on a floured surface until it is ¼ inch thick. Use a 1-inch bone-shaped cookie cutter to cut out shapes. Transfer them to a baking sheet lined with parchment paper.

4. Bake for 15 minutes, until the cookies are hard and just beginning to brown at the edges.

5. Cool completely and serve to your doggy!

Basic FROSTING

This frosting can be piped just like buttercream! It does dry differently and can crack overnight, so I recommend decorating with it on the same day you plan on serving it.

16 ounces cream cheese, room temperature

¾ cup (6 ounces) creamy peanut butter

1. Place the cream cheese and peanut butter in a large bowl and beat with an electric mixer until smooth and fluffy.

2. Store covered, at room temperature, until ready to use.

TREACLE TIP: *This doesn't have the same sugar content as human buttercream does, but it is still high in calories, so it's best to use it sparingly when decorating cakes or cupcakes for your pup.*

Pupparazzi

Everyone has their awkward moments on camera, including Paddington and Treacle. Here are some hilarious photos that haven't made it onto their Instagram feeds!

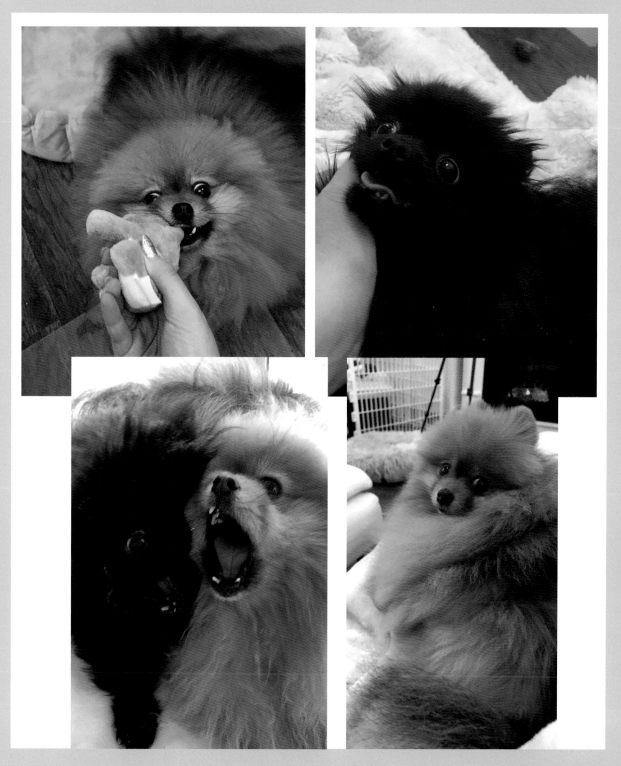

SPRING

Springtime
SANDWICH COOKIES

These cookies are so dainty and perfect for spring! We're using a twist on my favorite dog cookie base, which contains peanut butter, pumpkin, and coconut.

———————————— MAKES 1 DOZEN SANDWICH COOKIES ————————————

Cookie Dough

4 eggs
1 cup plain canned pumpkin
½ cup liquid coconut oil
½ cup peanut butter
1½ cups organic coconut flour
2 tablespoons turmeric
½ teaspoon baking soda

Filling

¼ cup peanut butter
1 dozen fresh raspberries

Make the cookies:

1. Beat the eggs lightly with an electric mixer. Add the pumpkin puree, coconut oil, and peanut butter and mix until well combined. Add the coconut flour, turmeric, and baking soda, and mix until fully incorporated.

2. Shape the dough into 2 balls, wrap in plastic wrap, and chill in the freezer until firm, about 20 minutes.

3. Preheat oven to 350°F. Roll each ball of dough out between 2 sheets of parchment paper. Cut out cookies with a 1-inch flower cookie cutter. Place the cookies on a baking sheet lined with parchment paper and use a round piping tip to cut the centers out of half the cookies. Bake 15 minutes. Cool completely.

Assembly:

1. Spread the whole cookies with some peanut butter and top with a center-less cookie.

2. Place a raspberry onto the center of the cookie and serve these to your dainty little pup! These cookies can be stored in the fridge for 3 to 4 days.

Baby Treacle's TEA PARTY

This was the first special recipe that I made for Treacle when she came home! These are three easy recipes than can be whipped up at a moment's notice, but still feel super special. Perfect for a puppy party!

Peanut Butter Bones
Bone cookies (page 41)
Peanut butter

Strawberry Cups
Strawberries
Plain yogurt
Blueberries

Raspberry Surprises
Raspberries
White cheddar cheese

Peanut Butter Bones
1. Place some peanut butter into a piping bag fitted with a small, star-shaped piping tip.

2. Pipe two dollops onto the top of each bone cookie.

Strawberry Cups
1. Slice out the top and hollow out the center of a strawberry. Slice a tiny bit off the tip of the strawberry, so that it sits upright like a cup.

2. Fill the strawberry cup with yogurt and top with a blueberry.

Raspberry Surprises
1. Chop some white cheddar cheese into tiny cubes.

2. Stuff a cube into the center of each raspberry.

TREACLE TIP: *Want to serve some tea at your tea party? Try some of our Homemade Broth (page 34) at room temperature!*

Fresh Fruit PUPPY PARFAITS

Paddington first showcased this recipe in New York City, where we were flown to host a doggy meet up! It was so much fun to share this recipe with other doggies. He did very well, especially considering that he was only five months old at the time!

───────────────── MAKES 3 SMALL PARFAITS ─────────────────

⅓ cup plain yogurt
1 apple slice, finely diced
1 mango slice, finely diced
3 slices of banana
2 strawberries, finely diced
3 blueberries
3 raspberries
Honey

1. Layer the sliced and chopped fruit into small cups, alternating the fruit with dollops of yogurt.

2. Top each with a blueberry and a raspberry, then drizzle with honey. Serve immediately to your puppy!

TREACLE TIP: *Raspberries are a wonderful "sometimes" treat. Raspberries are an excellent source of vitamin C, K, B-complex, fiber, and minerals such as iron, folic acid, copper, magnesium, potassium, and manganese. The risk of raspberries is that they contain the highest levels of natural xylitol, which is very toxic to dogs. Raspberries can be eaten, but only in moderation. Paddington and I only have one or two raspberries at a time, but I recommend checking with your vet first.*

Mini BLUEBERRY MUFFINS

I receive many questions on Instagram and YouTube about whether blueberries in dog recipes are safe—yes, they are safe! The only risk is their size, as they are a potential choking hazard, especially if frozen. However, you don't have to worry in this recipe, as they are baked into the muffins and soften significantly during baking.

———————————— MAKES 2 DOZEN MINI MUFFINS ————————————

1 banana, mashed
1 tablespoon honey
1 egg
2 tablespoons olive oil
½ cup whole wheat flour
1 teaspoon baking powder
½ cup quick cooking oats
1 cup fresh or frozen blueberries

TREACLE TIP: *Be sure to remove the paper cupcake liner before serving to your dog. The liner makes it much easier to prevent the muffins from sticking to the cupcake pan, but no doggy wants to eat paper . . . well, maybe they do, but best to avoid it!*

1. Preheat oven to 350°F.

2. In a large bowl, combine the banana, honey, egg, and olive oil. In a separate bowl, combine the flour, baking powder, and oats. Add this to the wet mixture and mix until combined.

3. Add the blueberries and gently fold into to mixture.

4. Spoon the batter into a lined mini cupcake tin.

5. Bake for 12 minutes, or until a skewer inserted into the muffins comes out clean. Cool completely. These muffins should be stored in the fridge and eaten within 3 to 4 days. These can also be stored in the freezer and thawed in the fridge overnight.

BIRTHDAY CAKE *for Dogs*

This was Paddington's first birthday cake! He loved it so much that he toppled it over and it got all over the floor. I figure that the more the mess, the more it's enjoyed!

8 ounces turkey bacon
2 cups whole wheat flour
1 tablespoon baking powder
1 cup light coconut milk
¼ cup olive oil
2 large eggs
½ cup cream cheese, room temperature
Mini carrots
Fresh strawberries
Blueberries

1. Preheat oven to 400°F.

2. Place the turkey bacon in a food processor and pulse until finely ground.

3. Pour the flour and baking powder into a large bowl and mix to combine. Add the bacon, coconut milk, oil, and eggs, and mix until well combined.

4. Pour the mixture into a greased baking sheet and smooth the surface. Bake for 25 to 30 minutes, until golden brown. Cool completely on the baking sheet.

5. Slice the cake into rounds. You can create as big a cake with as many layers as you like! Any leftover cake can be chopped into small pieces and used as treats.

6. Stack the layers on top of each other, spreading 1 tablespoon of cream cheese between each layer. Then coat the entire cake in a thin layer of cream cheese. Slice the mini carrots into thin sticks—we'll use these as candles! Create as many carrot candles as you need for your dog's birthday.

7. Decorate the cake with the candles, strawberries, and blueberries. Slice your dog a small slice and enjoy!

Iced EASTER COOKIES

This icing technique is very easy and uses all natural ingredients. If you have human babies and fur babies, these are the perfect cookies to decorate together.

— MAKES ABOUT 50 TO 60 SMALL COOKIES —

Cookie Dough
⅔ cup plain canned pumpkin
¼ cup natural peanut butter
2 large eggs
2½ cups whole wheat flour, plus
    extra for dusting your surface

Icing
¼ cup cream cheese
3–5 fresh raspberries
3–5 fresh blackberries
Turmeric powder

Bake the cookies:
1. Preheat oven to 350°F.

2. Place the pumpkin puree, peanut butter, and eggs in a large bowl and beat with an electric mixture until well combined, about 1 to 2 minutes.

3. Add the flour, beating until just combined. If the mixture is too dry, add up to ¼ cup of water.

4. Transfer the dough to a floured surface and knead a couple times until it comes together. Roll the dough out to ¼-inch-thick and cut out with mini Easter cookie cutters.

5. Place the cookies on a baking sheet lined with parchment paper and bake for 20 to 25 minutes, or until the edges are golden brown. Transfer to a wire rack and cool completely.

Make the icing:
1. Melt the cream cheese in the microwave for 5 to 10 seconds, until it has a yogurt-like consistency. Then divide into 3 bowls to dye different colors.

2. To make pink icing, microwave the raspberries until bubbling, about 10 seconds. Strain to remove any seeds. Add a couple drops to the cream cheese. Use the same technique with the blackberries for purple icing. For yellow icing, add a pinch of turmeric powder to the cream cheese.

3. Spread onto the cookies and enjoy!

Crisp VEGGIE SALAD

This salad is great for those looking to incorporate more fresh veggies into their dog's diet, or if you are on the hunt for low-calorie treats. This salad isn't a meal, per se; more like a little buffet to offer your pups when they are in the mood to snack. These veggies are packed with a variety of vitamins and minerals. More information on each vegetable can be found in the Food Safety Guide on page 3.

———————————————— MAKES 1 SNACK BOWL ————————————————

Sugar snap peas, sliced in half
   diagonally
Mini cucumbers, sliced into rounds
Carrots, cut with a mini cookie cutter
Red, orange, and yellow bell pepper,
   cut into 1-inch pieces
Fresh parsley (curly parsley is
   preferable over flat Italian parsley)
Frozen green peas, thawed
Celery, cut into diagonal 1-inch pieces

1. Simply arrange the veggies in your dog's food bowl and welcome them to take their pick!

CARROT CAKE *for Dogs*

Carrots are great for dogs! They are very low in calories, high in fiber, and packed full of vitamin A.

MAKES 1 (4-INCH) ROUND CAKE

1 cup grated carrots (approx. 1 large carrot)

1 large egg

½ cup canned sardines, drained and shredded

¼ cup sunflower seed oil

¼ cup water

1 cup whole wheat flour

Cooking spray

1½ cups cream cheese, room temperature

Sliced carrot, for decoration

1. Preheat the oven to 350°F.

2. Combine the grated carrot and egg in a bowl and beat until well combined. Add the sardines, sunflower seed oil, and water, and mix until combined. Add the flour and mix well.

3. Spray two 4-inch round cake pans with cooking spray and divide the batter between them, smoothing the surface. Place on a baking sheet and bake for 35 minutes, until golden brown on top. Cool completely in the pans.

4. Beat the cream cheese with an electric mixer until pale and fluffy.

5. Slice each cake in half to create a total of 4 layers. Place one layer on a serving tray of your choice and spread 2 tablespoons of cream cheese over the surface. Repeat with the remaining layers. Cover the entire surface sparingly with cream cheese—they shouldn't eat too much cream cheese, so just use enough to give the cake a white appearance. Place the remaining cream cheese in a piping bag fitted with a small star-shaped piping tip and pipe dollops of cream cheese onto the top of the cake.

6. Place pieces of sliced carrot onto each dollop and serve!

Love Is Love GUMMIES

Enjoy pride with your pup! Pride treats can be tricky for dogs, because finding dog-safe food coloring is a bit of an adventure. After some trial and error, I've managed to create the (almost!) entire rainbow. Some additional colorings can be blue spirulina for a deeper blue and carob powder for brown.

— MAKES ABOUT 20 TO 25 (1-INCH) GUMMIES —

2 cups chicken broth (page 37)
6 tablespoons gelatin

Natural coloring options:
Red/pink—beet powder
Orange—beet powder and ground turmeric
Yellow—ground turmeric
Light green—green spirulina and ground turmeric
Teal—green spirulina
Purple—beet powder and green spirulina

1. Place the chicken broth in a small pot. Sprinkle the gelatin on top, whisk it into the chicken broth, and allow it to develop for 5 minutes. Set the pot to medium heat and whisk until the gelatin has fully dissolved.

2. Divide the liquid into as many bowls as you like. Add pinches of each powder according to the colors you would like to make. Start with just a pinch of powder and slowly increase the amount until you achieve the color you like.

3. Pour the jelly into square or shallow trays and place them in the fridge to set, about 1 to 2 hours.

4. Gently unmold the jellies and use a small cookie cutter to cut out hearts. Serve them to your pup! To store, place them in a plastic container and keep in the refrigerator for 2 to 3 days.

Paw Print COOKIES

These cookies are packed with nutrient-dense seeds and are a delightful cakey texture. They were so popular while shooting this cookbook that we ran out before I had the chance to freeze any!

— MAKES 30 COOKIES —

2 large eggs
½ cup plain canned pumpkin
¼ cup liquid coconut oil
¼ cup peanut butter
¾ cup organic coconut flour
¼ teaspoon baking soda
1 tablespoon whole flax seeds
1 tablespoon ground flax seeds
1 tablespoon chia seeds
90 individual carob chips
    (about 1 cup)
¼ cup carob chips for melting

TREACLE TIP: *Carob is a dog-safe chocolate alternative! It's great to use for cookie decorating.*

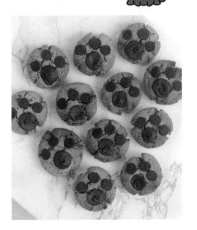

1. Preheat the oven to 350°F.

2. In a large bowl, combine the eggs, pumpkin, coconut oil, and peanut butter with an electric mixer.

3. In a separate bowl, combine the coconut flour, baking soda, whole and ground flax seeds, and chia seeds. Add this to the wet mixture and mix with an electric mixer until just combined.

4. Roll the dough into tablespoon-sized balls. Gently flatten each ball of dough into a patty and place on a baking sheet lined with parchment paper.

5. Use a skewer or chopstick to poke 3 holes into the cookies for the toes. Use your finger to create an indentation on the center of the paw.

6. Place the carob chips point side down onto the cookies as the toes. The holes should make it easy to place the pointed ends of the carob chips. Leave the palms bare at this point.

7. Bake the cookies for 15 minutes, until the edges are beginning to brown.

8. Place the remaining carob chips in a microwave-safe bowl and microwave for 30-second intervals, fully mixing at each interval, until fully melted.

9. Place a dollop of melted carob onto the palm of each paw, completing the paw prints.

10. Allow to cool completely before giving to your pup!

Classic COOKIE FROSTING

You know those adorable frosting cookies at pet stores? I've been admiring them for years, yet the only recipes I could find online for dog-safe frosting are an endless list of ingredients that I've never heard of. I thought that I was out of luck, when I made a discovery while shooting this cookbook! You can get the same look, in a piping bag-friendly consistency, with just two ingredients. Get your pups ready, because it's time to cute-ify their snacks!

——————————— ENOUGH TO DECORATE 4 TO 5 (3-INCH) COOKIES ———————————

1 cup yogurt chips
1 teaspoon liquid coconut oil
Powdered food coloring (see page 65
    for list of safe colors)

TREACLE TIP: *Make sure to check that there are no artificial sweeteners in your yogurt chips before purchasing. They are toxic to us doggies!*

1. Place the yogurt chips in a microwave-safe bowl and microwave for 30-second intervals until melted, stirring at each interval.

2. The yogurt can be quite thick at this stage, so the addition of coconut oil helps to thin it out enough to decorate the cookies easily. Add the coconut oil very gradually until your desired consistency is achieved.

3. Divide the yogurt into as many bowls as colors you'd like to use. Dye the yogurt your desired colors with powdered food coloring. Start with a pinch of coloring and add more until your desired color is achieved.

4. To decorate, you can dunk the cookies directly into the yogurt or use a piping bag and a small, round piping tip to create more detailed decorations. Allow the yogurt to dry between applying colors. It dries pretty quickly, so you should only need to wait 10 to 15 minutes.

5. Once the cookies are decorated, let them sit about 1 hour at room temperature for the yogurt to fully set. Then give them to your sweet doggy!

Paddington's SWEET POTATO & CHICKEN TWISTS

These were Paddington's first treats when I brought him home as a puppy! We did start with a store-bought version, so it warms my heart that I'm now able to make them for him at home now. They were his "bedtime cookie" that he ate in his crate, which was a routine he loved. One afternoon, I gave him one of these cookies and he was so confused because it wasn't bedtime! He made the saddest little distressed sound until I brought his crate into the living room and he happily enjoyed his cookie in his crate.

———————————— MAKES ABOUT 1 DOZEN TWISTS ————————————

1 large sweet potato
1–2 chicken breasts

TREACLE TIP: *For some extra flavor, sprinkle some fresh, chopped curly parsley onto the twists before baking.*

1. Preheat oven to 200°F.

2. Prepare a large baking sheet lined with foil. Place the meat on an oven-safe cooling rack and place on top of the baking sheet. The rack will allow the meat to dry evenly on all sides, while the baking sheet will catch any drippings and keep your oven clean!

3. Cut the sweet potato into 4-inch-long batons, about ½-inch-thick.

4. Slice the chicken into long, thin strips. Wrap the chicken around the sweet potato sticks and place them on the cooling rack.

5. Bake the twists for 3 to 4 hours, until the meat looks and feels dry.

6. Remove the treats from the oven and cool completely.

7. To store, keep in a paper bag in the fridge or freezer. Using a paper bag instead of a plastic sandwich bag will ensure that the meat stays dry and does not collect moisture. They can be stored in the fridge for up to 3 weeks and the freezer for up to 3 months.

BREATH FRESHENING
Treats

Parsley is a great breath freshener for dogs and is a natural source of vitamins A, C, and K. It also has anti-inflammatory and antimicrobial properties, which promote good kidney and urinary health. Be sure to use the curly variety when using it as an ingredient (instead of a garnish), as it is healthier for dogs than flat Italian parsley.

—————————————— MAKES 5 (2-INCH) TREATS ——————————————

½ apple
1 cup plain yogurt
1 tablespoon loosely packed fresh
    mint leaves, finely chopped
3 tablespoons loosely packed fresh
    parsley leaves, finely chopped

1. Grate the apple with a cheese grater. Place this in a medium size bowl and add the yogurt, mint, and parsley.

2. Spoon the mixture into a silicone mold of your choice. Place the mold in the freezer for 3 to 4 hours, or until it is frozen solid.

3. Give one to your pup and enjoy a break from doggy breath!

TREACLE TIP: *Does your dog need to whiten their teeth as well? Add some diced strawberries, which have teeth-whitening properties!*

NYC BLACK & WHITE
Cookies

New York City is my absolute favorite, so I had to share this love with my dogs. These cookies are a spin on NYC's classic Black and White Cookies. While the human version have a slightly cakey consistency, your puppy won't complain, thanks to the bacon and cheddar cheese!

———————————— MAKES ABOUT 1 DOZEN (2-INCH) COOKIES ————————————

4 strips bacon, uncooked
1½ cups quick oats
½ cup grated cheddar cheese
2 large eggs
¼ cup yogurt chips
½ teaspoon coconut oil, divided
¼ cup carob chips

TREACLE TIP: *Make sure you are using carob chips—never chocolate chips! Carob is a dog-safe alternative to chocolate, and melts in a very similar way. Also check the ingredients on your yogurt chips to ensure that they don't contain any artificial sweeteners!*

1. Preheat the oven to 350°F. Cook the bacon in a pan set to medium heat. Once the bacon is crispy, move to a paper towel to absorb any excess oil. Allow to cool completely, then break into rough pieces.

2. Place the oats in a food processor and pulse until they have ground into a powder. This is a quick way to create a "flour"! Add the cheddar cheese and bacon to the food processor and pulse until all ingredients have been combined and processed together to create a delicious cheesy, meaty flour.

3. Place the flour mixture in a large bowl and add the eggs. Beat with an electric mixer until thoroughly combined. This dough is a little dense, but quite easy to work with.

4. Roll the dough out between 2 sheets of parchment paper until it is ¼-inch thick. Cut out 2-inch round circles with a cookie cutter and place on a baking sheet lined with parchment paper. Bake for 15 to 20 minutes, or until the edges are golden. Cool completely.

(Continued)

5. Place the yogurt chips into a microwave-safe bowl and microwave for 30-second intervals, mixing at each interval, until fully melted. Add about ¼ teaspoon of coconut oil and mix well. This will give a smooth, velvety consistency that is easy to decorate with.

6. Dunk the cookies halfway into the yogurt. Use the edge of the bowl to scrape off any excess yogurt and return the cookies to the baking sheet for the yogurt to set, about 1 hour.

7. Once the yogurt has set, place the carob chips in a microwave-safe bowl, also heating at 30-second intervals until fully melted. Add ¼ teaspoon coconut oil and mix well. Dip the opposite sides of the cookies into the carob, scraping off the excess and allowing the cookies to set on a baking sheet, about 1½ hours.

8. Serve to your pup and give them a taste of the big apple!

Puppicorn CAKE

What is more magical than a unicorn? A puppicorn, of course! Unleash your dog's wildest fantasies with this adorable apple-cheddar puppicorn cake!

—————————————— MAKES 1 (6-INCH) CAKE ——————————————

Cake Base

3 cups whole wheat flour
½ cup quick cooking oats
4 teaspoons baking powder
1 teaspoon baking soda
1 cup unsweetened applesauce
½ cup coconut oil, extra for the pan
2 tablespoons maple syrup
2 tablespoons honey
4 large eggs
2 cups grated apple
1 cup grated cheddar cheese

Decorations

1 batch of cookie dough—can be any
   recipe in this book!
1 cup yogurt chips
1 teaspoon liquid coconut oil
1 teaspoon turmeric
1 teaspoon beet powder

Assembly

2 batches Basic Frosting (page 43)
1 tablespoon carob powder
1 teaspoon ground turmeric
¼ cup carob chips, for melting,
   + 6 extra carob chips
Treacle's Training Treats (page 33)

Bake the cake:

1. Preheat the oven to 350°F.

2. Combine the flour, oats, baking powder, and baking soda in a bowl. Set aside. In a large bowl, combine the remaining ingredients with an electric mixer.

3. Grease three 6-inch pans with coconut oil. Divide the cake batter between the pans and smooth the surface. Bake for 25 to 30 minutes, or until a skewer inserted into the cakes comes out clean. Cool completely.

Make the puppicorn horn and ears:

1. Roll your cookie dough out between 2 sheets of parchment paper. Use a sharp knife to cut out the shape of a double-ended unicorn horn and ears (half of the cookie will be inserted into the cake).

2. Place on a baking sheet lined with parchment paper. Bake according to the cookie recipe, adding a couple extra minutes due to the large size. Cool completely.

3. Melt the yogurt chips in a microwave-safe bowl for 30 second intervals, stirring at each interval, until melted. Gradually add the coconut oil, until you achieve a smooth consistency.

(Continued)

4. Spread the yogurt onto the entire surface of the ears and horn. Set aside for about 30 minutes.

5. Pour about ½ of the remaining yogurt into a bowl and dye it yellow with the turmeric. Pour it into a piping bag fitted with a small, round piping tip. Pipe the details of the horn. Pour the remaining yellow yogurt into a bone-shaped silicone mold. Set aside.

6. Add the beet powder to the remaining yogurt and stir to combine. Use this to create the pink inner ears. Allow all cookies to set for about 1 hour.

Decorate the cake:

1. Use a serrated knife to smooth the tops of the cakes. Stack the cakes, spreading ¼ cup of frosting between each layer. Coat the cake in an even, thin layer of white frosting. Set aside 1 cup of white frosting. Dye the remaining frosting beige by adding the carob powder and ground turmeric.

2. Spread the beige frosting onto the cake and create your desired fur patterns. Take the remaining beige and white frosting and spread both colors vertically into a piping bag fitted with a large, star-shaped piping tip. The piping bag should appear to have a different color on each side. Set aside.

3. Carve vertical openings in the top of the cake and stick the horn and ears into the cake. Using the piping bag from the previous step, pipe swirls and dollops of frosting all around the head, ears, and horn.

4. Unmold the yogurt bones and place them in the curly fur on the sides of the cake. Repeat with some training treats.

5. Melt the carob chips in a microwave safe bowl for 30-second intervals, stirring at each interval, until melted. Place a square of parchment paper on a flat surface. Use a small spoon to draw 2 large circles for the eyes and a heart for the nose. Allow to fully set, about 1 hour. Stick the eyes and nose onto the cake. Use the remaining 6 carob chips to create the dog's cheeks. Lastly, use a knife or skewer to etch the mouth into the cake.

6. This cake is best served fresh, but leftovers can be stored in the fridge for 3 to 4 days or frozen for up to 3 months. I like to freeze Paddington and Treacle's birthday cakes and thaw them slice by slice to use as treats.

TREACLE TIP: *This frosting tends to crack when left overnight, so make sure to decorate the cake a couple hours before serving (and taking photos!).*

Morning Walkies CREAM CHEESE & "LOX" BAGELS

I've discovered that there are very few things more adorable than seeing a dog carrying a mini bagel in its mouth. It's like the dog is on its way to work. Where do you work, puppy? Are you picking up the newspaper and your morning bone broth along the way? Did you remember to bring your briefcase? Why do you need a briefcase?

—————————— MAKES ABOUT 2 DOZEN MINI BAGELS ——————————

Bagels
2 bananas, mashed
2 tablespoons maple syrup
1 large egg
½ cup low-fat milk
2½ cups whole wheat flour
1 teaspoon baking powder
Coconut oil, for pan

Filling
½ cup cream cheese, room
    temperature
2 cans of salmon in water, drained and
    rinsed

TREACLE TIP: *Bagels and lox typically use smoked salmon; however smoked salmon isn't healthy for dogs. That's why we're using canned salmon in this recipe!*

Bake the bagels:
1. Preheat the oven to 325°F.

2. In a large bowl, combine the bananas, syrup, egg, and milk. Add the flour and baking powder and mix until just combined.

3. Grease a mini doughnut pan with the coconut oil. Place the dough in a piping bag and snip off the tip to create a medium-sized hole. Pipe a ring of dough into each crevice in the pan.

4. Bake for 15 minutes, until the surfaces are lightly browned and the bagels are fully cooked. Allow to cool completely.

Assembly:
1. Slice the bagels in half horizontally.

2. Combine the cream cheese and salmon in bowl. Spread the mixture between both sides of the bagel and serve to your dog!

3. The bagels and filling are best stored separately in the fridge, as the bagels can get soggy if you pre-fill them. Both last about 3 to 4 days in the fridge, and the bagels can also be frozen for up to 3 months.

Catch of the Day
SALMON FISHCAKES

These fishcakes are packed with vitamins, minerals, and healthy fats. They are a great snack, but can also be crumbled into your dog's main food dish as a special little "extra" from time to time.

--- MAKES 16 FISHCAKES ---

2 (6-ounce) cans skinless and boneless salmon (in water), drained and rinsed
½ red bell pepper, finely chopped
1 stalk of celery, finely chopped
8 sugar snap peas, finely chopped
2 tablespoons fresh parsley, finely chopped
½ cup plain, unseasoned breadcrumbs
2 large eggs, lightly beaten
Liquid coconut oil, for brushing

1. Preheat the oven to 400°F.

2. Place all ingredients, except the coconut oil, in a large bowl and mix well.

3. Shape the mixture into patties and place on a baking sheet lined with parchment paper.

4. Brush the tops of the patties with coconut oil.

5. Bake for 15 minutes, or until golden brown. Cool completely before serving to your dog.

Weekend Brunch
EGGS ON "TOAST"

It's time for brunch with your best buddy! These fun cookies look just like eggs on toast and will be thoroughly enjoyed by your fur baby.

———————— MAKES ABOUT 20 "TOASTS" ————————

1 teaspoon honey
⅔ cup plain canned pumpkin
¼ cup peanut butter
2 large eggs
2½–3 cups rice flour
1 cup whole flax seeds
20 quail eggs (1 per "toast")
1 tablespoon coconut oil
A pinch of ground flax seeds, as "pepper" garnish

1. In a large bowl, combine the honey, pumpkin, peanut butter, and eggs with an electric mixer. Gradually add the rice flour until the dough comes together nicely. You may not need all of the flour.

2. Divide the dough into 2 balls. Shape it into 2 long rectangles, about 1-inch thick. Roll these rectangles of dough through the whole flax seeds. These seeds will make the sides of the toast appear like the toast crust! Wrap the dough in plastic wrap and chill in the freezer for 1 hour, until firm.

3. Preheat the oven to 350°F.

4. Unwrap the chilled dough and slice it into ¼-inch-thick "toasts." Place them on a baking sheet lined with parchment paper and bake for 10 minutes, until the edges begin to brown. Cool completely.

5. When ready to serve, fry the quail eggs. Drizzle some coconut oil onto a frying pan and set it to medium heat. Gently crack the quail eggs onto the pan and cook until the egg whites have fully cooked and the yolk is starting to set, about 3 to 5 minutes.

6. Gently place the eggs onto the "toast." Top with some ground flax seeds to look like "pepper" and serve to your pups!

Insta-Ready
SMOOTHIE BOWL

Is your fur-baby on Instagram? If so, they need this on their feed! Treat your pup like the fabulous influencer that they are with a decadent smoothie bowl.

—————————————— MAKES 2 CUPS OF SMOOTHIE ——————————————

1 banana, frozen
1 cooked beet, roughly chopped and
   frozen
¼ cup plain yogurt
2 tablespoons flax seeds

About 1 spoon of each topping you like:

Dragon fruit, cut into cubes
Fresh blueberries
Sugar snap peas
Sliced hard-boiled eggs
Yogurt Bones (from Furmaid Cake,
   page 129)
Unsweetened coconut shavings
Unsalted peanuts, finely chopped

1. Place the banana, beet, yogurt, and flax seeds in a blender and pulse until very smooth.

2. Spoon this into a little bowl and top with your dog's favorite ingredients. You can use anything that your dog likes!

3. This is best served right away, but the toppings can be prepped in advance.

TREACLE TIP: *Let's be friends on Instagram! Follow me @treacle_pom and @paddington_pom*

Meet Me in Paris
MADELEINES

If you've always dreamed of going to France, now you can bring your pup on a gastronomic tour!

———————————— MAKES ABOUT 1 DOZEN MADELEINES ————————————

1 cup whole wheat flour
¼ cup quick oats
2 teaspoons baking powder
¼ cup plain canned pumpkin
¼ cup peanut butter
½ cup applesauce
¼ cup coconut oil, plus extra for the
    pan
2 large eggs
1 carrot, grated

1. Preheat the oven to 350°F.

2. Combine the flour, oats, and baking powder in a medium-sized bowl. In a separate bowl, combine the pumpkin, peanut butter, applesauce, coconut oil, eggs, and carrot with an electric mixer.

3. Add the dry mixture and mix until just combined.

4. Lightly grease a madeleine pan with coconut oil. Spoon the batter into the pan and bake for 15 to 20 minutes.

5. Allow the madeleines to cool completely, then take your pup on a Parisian picnic!

TREACLE TIP: *If your dog is tiny, try using a mini madeleine pan!*

Prepped Puppy OVERNIGHT CHIA PUDDING

Chia seeds are rich in omega-3 fatty acids, so are a great alternative for dogs who are sensitive to fish and fish oil. They are also a great source of fiber, manganese, copper, and zinc.

——————————————— MAKES 1 CUP OF PUDDING ———————————————

2 tablespoons chia seeds
¼ cup plain yogurt
¼ cup chicken broth (page 37)
1 teaspoon honey
1 teaspoon salmon oil (optional)
¼ cup each chopped mango and
    blueberries

1. Pour the chia seeds, yogurt, chicken broth, honey, and salmon oil into bowl. Mix well, then let sit for 2 to 3 minutes. Mix again until there is no clumping.

2. Pour the pudding into a jar, seal, and refrigerate for 2 to 3 hours, or up to overnight.

3. Spoon the pudding into individual bowls. Top with mango and blueberries and let your pup enjoy!

TREACLE TIP: *No salmon oil on hand? Substitute it with coconut oil!*

Puppy Dog POCKY

Pocky, also known as Pepero, are a popular snack in Asia. Here is a dog-safe version, substituting the usual chocolate for dog-safe carob and yogurt chips. We're also adding some flax seeds, a good source of fiber as well as omega-3 fatty acids, which are excellent for your dog's coat and skin.

—————————— MAKES 60 TO 70 POCKY ——————————

1 teaspoon honey
⅔ cup plain canned pumpkin
¼ cup peanut butter
2 large eggs
2½–3 cups rice flour
1 cup carob chips
1 cup yogurt chips
Approx. 2 tablespoons liquid
    coconut oil
2 tablespoons flax seeds

1. Preheat oven to 350°F.

2. In a large bowl, combine the honey, pumpkin, peanut butter, and eggs with an electric mixer. Gradually add the rice flour until the dough comes together nicely. You may not need all of the flour.

3. Roll the dough out between 2 sheets of parchment paper so that it is ¼-inch thick.

4. Cut the dough into ½-inch-wide strips, then cut each strip into 3-inch-long sections. Transfer the pocky to a baking sheet lined with parchment paper.

5. Bake for 10 minutes, until the edges begin to brown. Cool completely.

6. To decorate, place the carob and yogurt chips into two separate microwave-safe bowls and microwave each for 30-second intervals, stirring at each interval, until fully melted. Add 1 tablespoon coconut oil to both the carob and yogurt and mix well. Place the carob and yogurt into piping bags fitted with small, round piping tips.

7. Pipe drizzles of yogurt and carob onto the pocky. For an extra touch, sprinkle some flax seeds on top. Allow the yogurt and carob to set completely, about 1 hour.

Biography of Paddington

First Name: Paddington

Middle Name: James

Birthday: July 14, 2016

Eye Color: Brown

Toenail Color: Mostly black, some white

Footpad Color: Black

Weight: 8 pounds

Favorite Foods: Salmon and sugar snap peas

Least Favorite Food: Pineapple

Nicknames: Little man, plumpus rumpus, Mr. Mac Paddingtons, fluffus puppus, tendie, porchetto, love monkey, Mr. Chonk, chonky chonk, fur baby, little monkey, puppy chow, chowder, sugar bear, nugget, love nugget, puppy nugget, chowdy chow, fluff nugget, pudding, sass nugget, love puppy, love puppy number 9, sausage, silly monkey, Paddingtonio, turducken, piggy, pig baby, doggy dog, Paddington pom, piggy poo, bubba gump, wiggly piggly, Mr. Peanut Butter, Mr. Pook

Signature Sleeping Position: On his back, legs pointing straight up into the air

Biography of Treacle

First Name: Treacle

Middle Name: Chestnut

Birthday: November 29, 2017

Eye Color: Dark brown

Toenail Color: Black

Footpad Color: Black

Weight: 3 pounds

Favorite Foods: Steak and honey

Least Favorite Food: Cranberries

Nicknames: Treacky treak, Miss muffin, little woman, fluffus puppus, Miss Chestnut, sweet tea, spicy tea, Treacle Von Chestnut, little beast, beast baby, little bean, snuggle monkey, porchetta, Treacle princess, fur baby, little chowder, sugar bean, little sausage, puppy chowder, love nut, fluff nut, sweetie sweet, grumpus, piggy, jelly bean, pig baby, little animal, piggy poo, Treacles, poppet, Treacle pickle, chupa chup, mcmuffin, pickleina, Treacleina, spirulina

Signature Sleeping Position: In a little ball

SUMMER

Let's Go to Doga
GREEN SMOOTHIES

After your downward and upward-facing dogs, it's time for a treat!

——————————— MAKES ABOUT 3 CUPS OF SMOOTHIE ———————————

1 cup water

2 fresh pears, peeled, cored, and roughly chopped

2 stalks of celery, chopped into 1-inch pieces

1 teaspoon fresh ginger, peeled and grated (using a cheese grater makes this so easy!)

½ fresh cucumber, not peeled, roughly chopped

1 cup frozen peas, thawed

¼ cup fresh mango, roughly chopped

1. Place all ingredients into a blender. Pulse until very smooth.

2. Pour the smoothie into little bowls for your dogs and enjoy!

TREACLE TIP: *This smoothie freezes very well, so pour the leftovers into an ice cube tray and use them as refreshing frozen treats!*

Freshly Baked PRETZELS

Pretzels are an adorable treat to give to your pup. These pretzels contain pumpkin, which aids in digestion and is helpful if your dog has an upset tummy. Peanut butter and coconut oil contain healthy fats that benefit your dog's skin, coat, and heart. And if Paddington's reaction is any clue, your fur baby will be begging for more!

—————————— MAKES 2 DOZEN PRETZELS ——————————

4 large eggs
1 cup plain canned pumpkin
½ cup solid coconut oil
½ cup peanut butter
1½ cups whole wheat flour
½ teaspoon baking soda
1 egg white, lightly beaten
Chia seeds (whole or milled), for
  sprinkling

1. Beat the eggs lightly with an electric mixer. Add the pumpkin, coconut oil, and peanut butter, and mix until well combined. Add the whole wheat flour and baking soda and mix until fully incorporated. Chill the bowl in the fridge for 1 hour.

2. Dust some flour over your work surface. Roll 2 tablespoons of dough out into a 12-inch-long rope. Shape into a pretzel by bending the rope into a V shape, then bringing the ends downwards and crossing them over themselves. Place the pretzel on a baking sheet lined with parchment paper. Repeat with the remaining dough and place the entire baking sheet in the freezer to chill until firm, about 20 minutes.

3. Preheat oven to 350°F. Brush the pretzels with the beaten egg white and sprinkle chia seeds on top.

4. Bake for 15 minutes. Cool completely.

Tropical BANANA POPSICLES

These popsicles are packed full of healthy fats and tons of vitamins and minerals. They also come with adorable bone "handles," which your dog can use to carry the popsicle to their desired snacking spot. Paddington and Treacle instinctively carried these by the handle and it was incredibly cute.

———————————— MAKES ABOUT 8 POPSICLES PER FLAVOR ————————————

Base
2 tablespoons melted coconut oil
1 banana
½ cup mango
1 tablespoon flax seeds

Choice of Flavoring
½ cup pineapple
½ cup frozen cranberries (or strawberries), thawed
½ cup frozen blueberries, thawed
Dog bone popsicle sticks (page 41, Treacle's Training Treats recipe, cut into bone shapes)

1. First, make the base. Place the coconut oil, banana, mango, and flax seeds in a blender or food processor and pulse until smooth.

2. Choose your dog's favorite flavoring and add this to the blender. Pulse again until smooth.

3. Pour the popsicle mixture into an ice cube mold. Stick bone shaped cookies into the popsicles as handles.

4. Freeze the popsicles for 2 to 3 hours, or until frozen solid. To unmold, run the underside of the ice cube tray under warm water, then gently twist it to release the popsicles.

Healthy GREEN BEAN CRISPIES

For those looking for a low-calorie training treat, this is it! Easy to make, delicious, and wonderfully crispy.

─────────────── MAKES 1½ TO 2 CUPS ───────────────

3 cups fresh green beans
½ tablespoon olive oil

1. Preheat oven to 170°F.

2. Toss the green beans in the olive oil.

3. Place on a baking sheet line with parchment paper. Bake for 8 hours. Turn the oven off and leave the green beans in the oven overnight.

4. Break into bite-sized pieces and enjoy!

> **TREACLE TIP:** *For an added benefit to your dog's skin and hair, use coconut oil instead of olive oil!*

Coconut SNOWBALL CAKE

I made this cake for Paddington's second birthday. He loves beef and because he is a Pomeranian, I always make sure to include coconut, which is great for his massive quantities of fluff! Be sure to use unsweetened coconut flakes, as the ingredients used for sweetening can be toxic to dogs.

─────────────── MAKES 1 (4-INCH) ROUND CAKE ───────────────

Cake Batter

7 medium red potatoes, peeled and diced
2 large eggs
¼ cup sunflower seed oil
¾ pound (12 ounces) ground beef
½ cup frozen blueberries
1 cup unsweetened shredded coconut
Cooking spray

Decorations

1 cup cream cheese, room temperature
1 cup unsweetened shredded coconut
Fresh blueberries
Fresh strawberries
Dog cookies

TREACLE TIP: *For easy homemade dog cookies to use for decoration, check out the Classic Dog Bones on page 41.*

Bake the cake:

1. Preheat oven to 375°F.

2. Place the potatoes in a pot and cover with water. Bring to a boil and boil until they are soft enough to be pierced with a knife, about 25 minutes. Drain and mash.

3. Place the eggs in a large bowl and beat with an electric mixer. Add the potatoes and sunflower oil and mix well. Add the beef and blueberries and mix well.

4. Spray a 9x9-inch baking pan with cooking spray and pour the batter into the pan. Smooth the surface and bake for 40 minutes, or until brown on top. Cool completely.

Decorate the cake:

1. Use a 4-inch round cookie cutter to cut out 3 rounds of cake. Slice each round in half.

2. Beat the cream cheese with an electric mixer until light and airy.

3. Stack the cakes and spread some cream cheese between each layer. Then coat the entire cake in a layer of cream cheese. Use the cream cheese sparingly, since dogs shouldn't have too much.

4. Press the shredded coconut onto the outside of the cake. Top the cake with fresh strawberries, blueberries, and dog cookies. Serve to your pups and enjoy!

Too Hot for Walkies
FRUITY FROZEN TREATS

These frozen yogurt treats are packed with vitamins and gut-healthy yogurt!

MAKES ABOUT 1 DOZEN TREATS

1 cup frozen blueberries, thawed
1 cup frozen strawberries, thawed
1½ cups plain yogurt

1. Spoon ⅓ of the yogurt into a silicone mold.

2. Divide the remaining yogurt in half and mix with the blueberries and strawberries.

3. Spoon the blueberry and strawberry yogurt into the remaining spaces in the silicone mold, then place in the freezer until frozen, about 2 to 3 hours.

4. Unmold and serve to your puppies on a warm day!

Pack for Puppy School
GRANOLA BARS

These granola bars are packed full of nutrients and vitamins to nourish your pup and get them ready to learn! We're using carob chips in this recipe, which are a dog-safe chocolate alternative. The presence of a chocolate chip-like ingredient can be jarring in dogs treats, but carob is perfectly safe. For more information as to why chocolate is harmful, check out the Food Safety Guide on page 3.

———————————— MAKES ABOUT 2 DOZEN BARS ————————————

1 cup quinoa flour

1 cup oat flour

½ cup milled flax seeds

1 cup whole flax seeds

1 large egg

1 cup low-fat milk

2 tablespoons real maple syrup

½ teaspoon baking soda

2 tablespoons unsweetened coconut flakes

¼ cup unsalted peanuts, finely chopped

¼ cup carob chips

1 tablespoon coconut oil, for greasing

1. Preheat oven to 350°F.

2. In a large bowl, combine all the ingredients, except for the coconut oil.

3. Cover a large baking sheet with parchment paper and drizzle the coconut oil on top to prevent sticking. Spoon the granola mixture onto the baking sheet. Use a rubber spatula to shape it into a 9x12-inch rectangle.

4. Use a large knife to score the mixture into 1-inch wide vertical strips, then each strip into 3 pieces, but don't cut all the way through. This way the granola bars can simply be broken into bars after baking.

5. Bake for 20 minutes, or until the edges are golden brown. Allow the granola bars to cool completely on the baking sheet, then gently bend the granola along the cuts you made to break it into bars.

6. These are best stored in the fridge for 4 to 5 days, or in the freezer for up to 3 months.

PUPSICLES

Popsicles with liver, broth, and fruit?! These are your dog's dream! Because these contain raw meat, I recommend giving these to your dog while outside, so you don't get any juices from the meat all over your home.

———————————— FILLS 1 ICE CUBE TRAY ————————————

¼ cup fresh blueberries
¼ cup fresh strawberries, chopped
2 tablespoons fresh curly parsley, roughly chopped
½ cup raw beef liver, cubed
2 cups homemade broth (page 34)
Baby carrots, 1 per pupsicle

1. Divide the blueberries, strawberries, parsley, and beef liver into an ice cube tray.

2. Top with some dog-friendly broth. Insert the carrots into the pupsicles to create edible handles.

3. Transfer to the mold to the freezer and chill until frozen, about 4 hours.

4. Unmold and give to your pup!

> **TREACLE TIP:** *If your dog is larger than us Pomeranians, you can use a popsicle mold instead of an ice cube tray! You should be able to get 4 regular-sized popsicles from this recipe. Remember to use regular carrots instead of mini carrots, as you'll need a much larger handle!*

Juicy Watermelon
GUMMY BONES

Watermelon is a fantastic treat for your dog, as it contains 92 percent water! It is also packed full of vitamins A, B$_6$, and C.

———————————— MAKES ABOUT 2 DOZEN GUMMIES ————————————

2 cups fresh watermelon, cubed, and seeds removed

2 tablespoon unflavored gelatin powder (*not* Jell-O)

¼ cup water

1. Place the watermelon in a food processor and pulse until smooth. Strain to remove any pulp. Measure 1 cup of watermelon juice.

2. Sprinkle the gelatin into the water and microwave for 15 to 30 seconds, until liquid.

3. Pour the liquid gelatin into the watermelon juice and mix well.

4. Pour the mixture into mini bone molds and place in the fridge until set, 1 to 2 hours.

5. Unmold and feed to your puppy! These gummies should be stored in the fridge and will last 4 to 5 days.

TREACLE TIP: *If your dog doesn't like watermelon, you can use strawberries, peaches, or cantaloupe!*

Rainbow BIRTHDAY CAKE

This cake was initially created for Paddington's third birthday! I added all his favorite ingredients: banana, peanut butter, and coconut! To achieve these rainbow colors, I purchased some powdered natural food coloring online and checked the ingredients to ensure that they were safe for dogs. For some ingredients that work fabulously as natural food coloring, check out the Love Is Love Gummies (page 65). The frosting I used pipes just like buttercream, but it is best used and consumed on the same day. It tends to crack when it dries out, so I recommended decorating the cake the same day of your parties and picture-taking.

─────────────── MAKES 1 (6-INCH) ROUND CAKE ───────────────

Cake Batter

8 cups unsweetened cornflakes

2 cups unsweetened coconut

2 cups whole wheat flour

1 cup peanut butter

2 cups hot water

2 bananas, mashed

4 large eggs

Cooking spray

Frosting & Decoration

16 ounces cream cheese, room
    temperature

¾ cup peanut butter

½ banana, roughly mashed

Natural food coloring powders (see
    page 65)

Classic Dog Bones (page 41)

2 tablespoons yogurt chips

Bake the cake:

1. Preheat oven to 325°F.

2. Place the cornflakes into a zip-top bag and crush into crumbs. Pour into a large bowl. Add the coconut flakes, flour, peanut butter, hot water, mashed banana, and eggs. Mix together with an electric mixer.

3. Spray 4 (6-inch) round cake pans with cooking spray. Divide the batter between the four pans. Bake for 40 minutes, until the edges are golden. Allow the cakes to cool completely.

(Continued)

Make the frosting:

1. Beat the cream cheese and peanut butter with an electric mixer until light and fluffy. Set aside.

2. Slice off any raised areas from the surface of the cakes with a serrated knife, so that the surfaces are flat.

3. Stack the cakes on a platter of your choice. Take 1 cup of frosting and mix it with the mashed banana. Spread the frosting evenly between each cake layer.

4. Divide half of the remaining frosting into 5 bowls. Dye one each red, yellow, green, blue, and pink with the natural food coloring. Place the frosting into piping bags and snip off the ends, creating a medium-sized tip. Place the remaining white frosting into a piping bag as well.

5. Pipe horizontal stripes onto the sides and top of the cake in the order of the rainbow, piping a white stripe between each layer. Use a cake spatula, or a cake scraper, to smooth the sides.

6. Top with extra dollops of frosting, dog treats, and yogurt chips. Serve to your puppy and enjoy!

TREACLE TIP: *For the multicolor swirl technique used on the dollops of frosting on the top of the cake, check out the Spooky Bones Cupcakes (page 151).*

Barking at the BBQ
CHEESEBURGERS

Your fur baby has always dreamed of receiving their very own burger. One that is just for them, no sharing involved. These burgers are a fabulous source of protein and fiber. The patties are mixed with Parmesan cheese, which acts as a binder but also a delicious surprise! Paddington loved these so much that he carried the burger bun around for an hour, "burying" it in several places.

— MAKES 12 BURGERS AND BUNS —

Burger Buns
2 large eggs
½ cup peanut butter
½ cup plain yogurt
½ cup honey
2 cups whole wheat flour
2 teaspoons baking soda

Patties
1 pound ground lamb, beef, chicken, or turkey
¼ cup frozen green peas, thawed
2 tablespoons grated Parmesan cheese
Liquid coconut oil, for the pan
1-inch square slices of cheddar cheese

Assembly
Plain yogurt, for the buns
Fresh parsley, as garnish

Bake the buns:

1. Preheat the oven to 350°F.

2. In a large bowl, combine the eggs, peanut butter, yogurt, and honey with an electric mixer. Add the flour and baking soda and mix until just combined.

3. Line a cupcake pan with silicone liners. These buns are quite dense, so silicone liners will make it much easier to remove them from the pan and prevent you from endlessly picking away paper cupcake liner from the sides of the bun. Divide the dough into the muffin tin wells. Bake for 18 to 20 minutes, until golden brown and a skewer inserted into the centers comes out clean. Cool completely.

Make the patties:

1. Combine the ground meat, green peas, and Parmesan cheese in a bowl. Mix until very well incorporated.

(Continued)

2. Shape the meat into 12 patties, flattening them so that they are just slightly larger than the buns. The patties will shrink during cooking, so this ensures that they will fit inside the buns nicely.

3. Set a frying pan to medium/medium-high heat. Drizzle coconut oil into the pan. Cook the patties for 3 to 4 minutes, until the bottoms are nicely browned.

4. Flip the patties and place a slice of cheddar cheese on top. Cook for an additional 3 to 4 minutes, until the cheese has melted and the meat is fully cooked. Cool completely.

Assembly:

1. Slice the buns in half and spread a thin layer of yogurt on the insides of the buns.

2. Place a patty between the buns and top with some parsley. Feed to your lucky puppy!

3. The patties should be stored in the fridge and eaten within 2 to 3 days. The buns can be made in advance and frozen, then thawed in the fridge overnight when needed.

Poolside PINEAPPLE PUPSICLES

This is a simple, but amazing recipe for hot summer days! Whether your pup is lounging by the pool or has just arrived home from a daily walkie, they will love these refreshing treats. Pineapple is packed full of vitamins, minerals, and fiber, and contains an enzyme called bromelain, which makes it easier for dogs to absorb proteins. Yogurt is great for gut health and blueberries round out this treat by providing antioxidants and phytochemicals, which help prevent cell damage in your pup.

——————————————— MAKES ABOUT 10 PUPSICLES ———————————————

1 fresh pineapple, peeled and cored
¼ cup fresh blueberries
½ cup plain yogurt

TREACLE TIP: *Don't stop at blueberries! You can combine strawberries, peaches, or melon with the yogurt for a variety of exciting fillings.*

1. Slice the pineapple into ½-inch-thick rounds. Place them on a baking sheet lined with parchment paper. Be sure that the baking sheet fits into your freezer.

2. Place the blueberries in a microwave-safe bowl and microwave for 10 to 20 seconds, until they begin to release their juices. Gently mash the blueberries until they are broken and juicy. This method releases the beautiful purple color in the berries!

3. Combine the yogurt and blueberries. Gently spoon this mixture into the center of the pineapples.

4. Place the baking sheet in the freezer for 1 to 2 hours, until the pineapple and yogurt filling is completely frozen. The pineapples can then be stacked in the freezer and stored in a more compact method.

$\mathscr{Treacle's}$ PRINCESS CAKE

This cake was Treacle's second birthday cake! She loves strawberries and fish, so I knew combining them into a pink princess cake was what it had to be. The beautiful pink frosting is dyed with beet puree, which not only creates a pretty color, but also packs the frosting with nutrients!

——————— MAKES 1 (6-INCH) ROUND TIERED CAKE ———————

Cake Batter

6 red beets, boiled and peeled
1 ripe banana, mashed
2 (5-ounce) cans tuna in water, drained
2 (5-ounce) cans salmon in water and without salt, drained
4 large eggs
1 cup hot water
1 cup sunflower seed oil, plus extra for the cake pans
4 cups whole wheat flour

Frosting

16 ounces cream cheese, room temperature
¾ cup peanut butter

Assembly

2 strawberries, finely diced
1 whole strawberry

Bake the cake:

1. Preheat oven to 350°F.

2. Place the beets in a food processor and pulse until they become a puree. Set aside 2 tablespoons of puree for the frosting.

3. Combine the remaining beet puree with the banana, tuna, salmon, and eggs, and mix well. Add the hot water and sunflower seed oil and mix well. Then add the flour and mix until just combined.

4. Grease 3 (6-inch) cake pans with extra sunflower seed oil. Divide the cake batter between the pans.

5. Bake for 40 minutes, or until the tops have browned and a skewer inserted into the centers comes out clean. Cool completely.

Make the frosting:

1. Beat the cream cheese and peanut butter with an electric mixer until light and fluffy. Set aside ¼ cup of frosting.

2. Add the reserved 2 tablespoons of beet puree to the remaining frosting and mix well.

(Continued)

Assembly:

1. Trim a thin layer off the tops of the cakes with a serrated knife. Then trim the sides of 2 cakes so that they get progressively smaller and create a 3-tier cake. You can save the scraps for treats!

2. Stack the cakes. Spread some pink buttercream between each layer and scatter some diced strawberries on top. Then coat the entire cake in a smooth layer of frosting.

3. Place the white frosting into a piping bag fitted with a small, star-shaped piping tip. Pipe dollops all around the cake. Top with a few swirls of frosting and a whole strawberry.

TREACLE TIP: *This frosting should be made, decorated with, and served the same day, as it can crack if left out overnight. For any leftover cake, simply cut it into cubes, pop into a freezer bag, and store in the freezer for treats!*

Furmaid CAKE

Dogs deserve just as special birthday cakes as humans do, and I'm sure that they would appreciate mermaids if they knew what they were. A fish that can also give cuddles? Paddington and Treacle are very interested.

1 batch of cookie dough—can be any recipe in this book that you choose!

1 cup yogurt chips

1 teaspoon liquid coconut oil

1 teaspoon blue spirulina powder

3-layer baked Apple Cheddar Cake base (recipe on page 77)

2 x Basic Frosting (recipe on page 43)

Treacle's Training Treats (page 33)

Make the mermaid tail and bone decorations:

1. Roll your cookie dough out between 2 sheets of parchment paper. Use a sharp knife to cut out the shape of a mermaid fin. Also make sure to extend the fin downward, so that there is enough cookie to be inserted into the cake.

2. Place the cookie fin on a baking sheet lined with parchment paper. Bake according to the cookie recipe, adding a couple extra minutes due to the large size of the fin. Cool the fin completely.

(Continued)

3. Melt the yogurt chips in a microwave safe bowl for 30-second intervals, stirring at each interval, until melted. Gradually add the coconut oil, only adding enough to achieve a smooth consistency.

4. Pour about ¼ of the yogurt into a bone-shaped silicone mold. Set aside. Add a pinch or two of blue spirulina to the remaining yogurt chips and stir to combine.

5. Spread the blue yogurt onto the mermaid fin. Set the fin aside for about 1 hour, for the yogurt to set.

Decorate the cake:

1. Use a serrated knife to smooth the tops of the cakes. Stack the cakes and spread ¼ cup of frosting between each layer. Use the same serrated knife to carve the cake into a rounded cone shape—like a mermaid tail!

2. Coat the cake in a thin layer of frosting. Dye the remaining frosting blue with some blue spirulina powder. Place the frosting in a piping bag fitted with a large, round piping tip.

3. Starting at the base of the cake, pipe a row of large dollops. Use a butter knife or offset baking spatula to drag each dollop upward, creating a scallop shape. Repeat over the entire surface of the cake, piping rows of dollops and spreading them upward.

4. Once the cake is fully covered, carve a vertical opening in the top of the cake and stick the mermaid fin into the opening. If the fin seems unstable, you can stick a couple straws or toothpicks behind the fin to help support it. Your doggy won't mind!

5. Unmold the yogurt bones and place them near the base of the fin, along with some training treats.

6. This cake is best served fresh, but leftovers can be stored in the fridge for 3 to 4 days or frozen for up to 3 months. I like to freeze Paddington and Treacle's birthday cakes and thaw them slice by slice to use as treats.

TREACLE TIP: *This frosting tends to crack when left overnight, so make sure to decorate the cake a couple hours before serving (and taking photos!).*

Boba TEA

I honestly don't think it gets any cuter than this! Doggies deserve boba tea just as much as you do—however theirs are much lower in sugar and very high in fiber. What flavor will your dog like best?

——————————— MAKES ABOUT 1 CUP PER FLAVOR ———————————

Pink
⅓ banana
⅓ cucumber, peeled
1 teaspoon liquid coconut oil
½ cup frozen cranberries, thawed (or strawberries)

Green
⅓ banana
⅓ cucumber, peeled
1 teaspoon liquid coconut oil
¼ cup honeydew melon
¼ cup finely chopped sugar snap peas

Purple
⅓ banana
⅓ cucumber, peeled
1 teaspoon liquid coconut oil
½ cup blueberries

Approx. ¼ cup blueberries per flavor, for the boba

> **TREACLE TIP:** *For some other flavors, you could add canned pumpkin, fresh cantaloupe, or pineapple!*

1. For whichever flavor you choose, place the banana, cucumber, coconut oil, and extra fruit/veggie into a blender or food processor and pulse until smooth.

2. Place some fresh blueberries into the bottom of your serving dish and top with the smoothie.

3. For a cute photo op, you can place a straw into the cup, but make sure to remove it before your dog starts eating.

50 Facts About Paddington

1. He prefers to sleep on the floor instead of on his many dog beds.

2. When it's time for walkies, he trots to the door and patiently lets us put his collar and harness on.

3. He can recognize the sound of a banana being peeled from several rooms away.

4. When I'm out on an errand, he waits by the front door the entire time.

5. His word for treats is "cookie."

6. When I bake him treats, he waits by the oven.

7. If he smells something yummy on the counter, he will walk around the kitchen on his hind legs like a human.

8. He prefers tiny dog toys.

9. He inspects every grocery bag that comes into the house.

10. When he's eating something extra delicious, his eyes will look in opposite directions.

11. He sneaks into the laundry basket and steals dirty laundry.

12. He tries to lick my legs after I put lotion on.

13. When I sit on the floor to film a video, he thinks it is playtime and will not leave me alone. There are puppy breaths in the background of all of my videos.

14. He is so used to being on camera that he will sit and pose when I'm holding my camera.

15. He loves everyone, except corgis.

16. He is a scavenger and always tries to sneak food from plates, cupboard, and garbage bins.

17. He "chunked out" at age three and became much more stocky. Not fat, just stocky!

18. He takes medicine so easily, just eats it right out of my hand! #legend

19. He always checks side tables in the living room for potential plates of food to lick.

20. If he wants a cookie, he stands up very straight and looks aggressively happy.

21. He tries to steal Christmas tree ornaments if they're hung on low branches.

22. He is scared of bikes.

23. He tries to mark every tree we pass on walkies, but his bladder is so tiny that it's usually just the marking "motion."

24. He snorts when he's excited.

25. He has been to New York City!

26. He once pooped in a department store.

27. He will bark if we leave a cereal box on the counter.

28. He learned the "hand pull" technique from Treacle and now does it more often than she does! See Treacle's 50 Facts if you want to know more!

29. He loves snow and will do zoomies in and out of the house on the first snow of the year.

30. He loves the classic Italian Christmas cake, Pandoro.

31. You can always hear his feet pitter-pattering as he trots through the house.

32. He gets kibble stuck between his cheek and teeth.

33. He likes to play in the water left after a shower.

34. He understands "come inside," but always squeezes in a few more barks before coming inside.

35. He is my boyfriend's sous chef in the kitchen when making dinner. He stands at his ankles and waits for any crumbs or scraps to fall.

36. He loves Australian shepherds. He met one when he was in puppy training school and it's been pure love ever since!

37. He likes to sleep in each morning, then takes another nap at noon.

38. He has a specific cry for salmon.

39. He loves walkies!

40. Paddington's doggy dad is the number-one Pomeranian show dog in Indonesia.

41. His doggy mom's name is Cairo and doggy dad's name is Patton.

42. He was the only puppy in his litter.

43. He used to like strawberries, but now spits them out if I give one to him.

44. He pretends that he can't get on the couch, in order to get us to lift him up.

45. He grunts in his sleep.

46. He secretly thinks that he's a big dog.

47. He only ever growls at corgis.

48. He will steal the dish towel if it's hanging low enough for him to grab.

49. When you say a word that he hasn't heard before, he will tilt his head and perk up his ears.

50. His fur color is officially called orange sable.

AUTUMN

Pumpkin PUP TARTS

I love making dog treats that have a surprise center, like these pop tarts. The look of awe on Paddington's face when he bites into these and realizes there is extra deliciousness inside . . . it's just so adorable.

─────────── MAKES ABOUT 1 DOZEN PUP TARTS ───────────

4 eggs
1½ cups plain canned pumpkin, divided
½ cup liquid coconut oil
½ cup peanut butter
1½ cups organic coconut flour
½ teaspoon baking soda
½ cup cream cheese

1. Beat the eggs lightly with an electric mixer. Add 1 cup pumpkin puree, coconut oil, and peanut butter and mix until well combined. Add the coconut flour and baking soda and mix until fully incorporated.

2. Shape the dough into 2 balls, wrap in plastic wrap, and chill in the freezer until firm, about 20 minutes.

3. Preheat oven to 350°F. Roll each ball of dough out between 2 sheets of parchment paper until ¼-inch thick. Cut out rectangles from the dough, around 3x1½-inches.

4. Place on a baking sheet lined with parchment paper. Place the extra ½ cup of pumpkin into a piping bag fitted with a round piping tip.

5. Pipe a dollop of pumpkin onto half of the rectangle, then fold it over and seal closed with a fork.

6. Bake for 15 minutes, then cool completely.

7. Place the cream cheese in a microwave-safe bowl and microwave for 30-second intervals until melted and very smooth. Spread the cream cheese onto the surface of each pop tart and serve to your pup!

8. Store the pop tarts in the fridge and consume within 5 days.

Beef, Chicken, and Salmon
JERKY

Protein is the core of a dog's diet, so these treats are both nutritious and delicious! It's also a wonderful feeling to be able to make a treat that I usually pick up at the pet store. I feel like Paddington and Treacle can definitely taste the difference. Paddington learned where the jerky was stored and set up camp, constantly crying for more.

——————— QUANTITY WILL DEPEND ON YOUR PARTICULAR CUT OF MEAT ———————

Semi-frozen steak, chicken breast, or boneless salmon filet

TREACLE TIP: *During prep time, slice the meat along the grain so that the jerky is extra chewy!*

1. Preheat the oven to 200°F. Trim and remove any visible fat from the meat.

2. Using a sharp knife, slice the meat into ¼-inch-thick, long slices. Make sure all pieces are the same size and thickness.

3. Prepare a large baking sheet lined with foil. Place the meat on an oven-safe cooling rack and place the rack on top of the baking sheet. This will allow the meat to dry evenly on all sides, while the baking sheet will catch any drippings and keep your oven clean!

4. Bake for about 2 hours, or until the meat is completely dried out. If the meat is still bendable and spongy, return it to the oven and continue drying until it is firm and dry. There can be no moisture in the jerky whatsoever, or it will lead to mold.

5. Once they are finished baking, remove from the oven and allow them to cool completely.

6. To store, keep the jerky in a paper bag in the fridge or freezer. Using a paper bag instead of a plastic sandwich bag will ensure that the meat stays dry and does not collect moisture. They can be stored in the fridge for up to 3 weeks and the freezer for up to 3 months.

Pawfect CHICKEN PASTA

Paddington was very perplexed by the shape of this pasta, as he'd never eaten anything like it before. I highly encourage you to make some pasta for your dog, if only for the adorable confusion they display when experiencing curly pasta for the first time.

———————————— MAKES 1½ CUPS OF PASTA ————————————

1 small beet
2 tablespoons water
2 pounds ground chicken
1 cup quinoa pasta, cooked according
    to package instructions

TREACLE TIP: *Can't find quinoa pasta? Try brown rice pasta instead!*

1. Place the beet in a pot, cover with water, and bring to a boil. Cook for 45 minutes, or until tender. Drain, then place in a food processor, along with the water, and pulse until smooth. Cool to room temperature.

2. Combine the beet mixture and ground chicken in a bowl.

3. Spoon on top of the pasta and serve!

Crunchy Leaf APPLE PIES

Autumn is such a cozy season, and your pup deserves to enjoy the fresh produce just as much as you do! They will love the fruity surprise in the middle of these adorable pie cookies.

— MAKES ABOUT 10 (2-INCH) PIES —

Dough
½ cup unsweetened applesauce
1 large egg
1 tablespoon molasses
1¾ cups brown rice flour
1 teaspoon ground ginger

Filling
1 apple, finely chopped
1 tablespoon unsweetened applesauce
Coconut oil, for brushing

TREACLE TIP: *Is your dog tiny like me? Make mini pies using a 1-inch round cookie cutter instead!*

Make the dough:
1. Preheat the oven to 350°F.

2. Combine the applesauce, egg, and molasses with an electric mixer. Add the brown rice flour and ginger and mix until just combined.

3. Roll the dough out on a floured surface. Use a 2-inch round cookie cutter to cut rounds out of the dough. Place half of the rounds on a baking sheet lined with parchment paper.

Make the filling:
1. In a small bowl, combine the chopped apple with the applesauce. Spoon about 1 teaspoon of the mixture onto the center of the cookies on the baking sheet. Place another cookie round on top and press the edges with your fingers to seal.

2. Use a fork to strengthen the seal around the edges of the cookies. Then use a very sharp knife to cut an "x" in the top of each cookie.

3. Brush the cookies with coconut oil, then bake for 15 minutes, or until the edges are beginning to brown.

4. Allow the cookies to cool completely, then serve to your pup! Store these in an airtight container in the fridge for up to 5 days.

Peanut Butter CAKE

Every doggy deserves a peanut butter cake! This cake is chock-full of peanut butter in every bite. Clearly Paddington couldn't stop himself and decided that he was going to be part of the photoshoot, if it meant that he could sneak in an early nibble.

———————————— MAKES 1 (6-INCH) ROUND CAKE ————————————

Cake Batter

1 cup plain canned pumpkin
½ cup unsweetened applesauce
2 tablespoons pure maple syrup
1 tablespoon honey
½ cup peanut butter
2 large eggs
¼ cup crushed, unsalted peanuts
2 tablespoons coconut oil, plus extra
    for pan
2 tablespoons whole chia seeds
1 cup whole wheat flour

Decoration

¼ cup yogurt chips
¼ teaspoon turmeric powder
Basic Frosting (page 43)
2 cups unsalted peanuts, crushed

> **TREACLE TIP:** *If you don't have a piping bag or piping tips, that's okay! You can use a plastic sandwich bag and snip a small hole in the corner as an easy substitute.*

Bake the cake:

1. Preheat oven to 350°F.

2. In a large bowl, combine the pumpkin, applesauce, syrup, honey, peanut butter, eggs, peanuts, and coconut oil with an electric mixer. Add the chia seeds and flour and mix until just combined.

3. Grease 3 (4-inch) round cake pans with coconut oil. Divide the batter between the pans and smooth the surface. Bake for 20 to 25 minutes, until a skewer inserted into the cakes comes out clean. Cool the cakes completely.

Decorate:

1. First, make the bone decoration. Place the yogurt chips in a microwave-safe bowl and microwave for 30-second intervals, mixing at each interval, until melted. Add the turmeric to create a golden color. Pour into a 1- or 2-inch silicone bone mold. Set aside for about 30 minutes.

2. Use a serrated knife to cut off the tops of the cakes and smooth the surface. Stack the cakes,

(Continued)

spreading about ¼ cup of frosting between each layer. Cover the cake in an even layer of frosting.

3. Cup the crushed peanuts in your hand and gently press them onto the sides of the cake.

4. Place the remaining frosting into a piping bag fitted with a large, star-shaped piping tip. Pipe 3 dollops on top of the cake and top with the yogurt bone.

Spooky Bones CUPCAKES

Halloween is such a fun time as a dog owner! We're making it extra fun for our pups with these delicious maple pumpkin cupcakes, topped with naturally colored frosting.

——————— MAKES 12 CUPCAKES ———————

Batter
1 cup quick oats
2 teaspoons baking powder
1 teaspoon ground ginger
2 large eggs
2 tablespoons maple syrup
2 tablespoons peanut butter
1 cup plain canned pumpkin
1 cup grated apple
½ cup plain yogurt
¼ cup flax seeds

Decorations
1 cup yogurt chips
1½ teaspoons ground turmeric, divided
1½ teaspoons beet powder, divided
Basic Frosting (recipe 43)
1 teaspoon blue spirulina

> **TREACLE TIP:** *If you can't get your hands on blue spirulina for the frosting, microwave 1 to 2 tablespoons of fresh blueberries and use the blueberry juice to dye the frosting!*

Bake the cupcakes:
1. Preheat oven to 350°F.

2. Place the oats in a food processor and pulse until it resembles flour. Add the baking powder and ginger and pulse a few more times until fully combined. Set aside.

3. In a large bowl, combine the eggs, syrup, peanut butter, pumpkin, apple, yogurt, and flax seeds with an electric mixer. Add the flour mixture and mix until just combined.

4. Spoon the batter into a lined cupcake pan. Bake for 35 to 40 minutes, or until a skewer inserted into the centers comes out clean. Allow the cupcakes to cool completely.

Make the decorations:
1. Place the yogurt chips in a microwave-safe bowl and microwave for 30-second intervals, stirring at each interval, until the chips have fully melted.

2. Divide the yogurt in half and dye one half orange by adding ½ teaspoon turmeric and ½ teaspoon beet powder. Leave the second bowl plain white.

(Continued)

3. Pour the white yogurt into a bone-shaped candy mold and the orange yogurt into a pumpkin-shaped candy mold. Set aside for the yogurt to set, about 30 to 45 minutes.

Assembly:

1. Divide the frosting in half. Add remaining 1 teaspoon turmeric to one half, dying it yellow. Add 1 teaspoon beet powder and 1 teaspoon blue spirulina to the remaining frosting, dying it purple.

2. Place a large, star-shaped piping tip into a piping bag. Spread the yellow frosting vertically into half of the piping bag. Fill the remaining half of the piping bag with the purple frosting. When holding the piping bag vertically, half should be yellow and half should be purple.

3. Pipe a swirl of frosting onto each cupcake. Top with a yogurt pumpkin and bone. Serve to your spooky Halloween puppy!

Paddington's PUMPKIN PIE

Welcome the cooler weather with these adorable peanut butter and pumpkin pies!

— MAKES 3 SMALL PIES —

1 large egg
¼ cup quick-cooking oats
2 tablespoons shredded mozzarella
    cheese
1 tablespoon peanut butter
⅛ cup hot water
¾ cup plain canned pumpkin
¼ cup cream cheese, room
    temperature

1. Preheat oven to 325°F.

2. Beat the egg well. Pour ¼ of the egg into a bowl. Add the oats, mozzarella cheese, peanut butter, and enough hot water to create a dough consistency.

3. Press the dough into 3 small oven-safe ramekins. Be sure to press it up the sides like a crust, leaving a well in the middle for filling. If you plan to remove the pies from the ramekins before serving, use silicone baking cups and lightly grease them with organic coconut oil before adding the dough.

4. Bake for 15 minutes. Cool completely.

5. Fill the pies with canned pumpkin. Place the cream cheese into a piping bag fitted with your desired piping tip (I used a #6B tip). Pipe a dollop of cream cheese onto the center of each pie and serve to your doggy!

Pup-kin Spice CUPCAKES

Pumpkin is a wonderful vegetable for dogs, which means that your dog is probably anticipating pumpkin spice season just as much as you are!

───────────────── MAKES 3 DOZEN CUPCAKES ─────────────────

2 large eggs
1 cup plain canned pumpkin
1 cup mashed banana
½ cup ground chicken
½ cup hot water
2 teaspoons ground ginger
2½ cups whole wheat flour
Cooking spray
½ cup cream cheese, room
    temperature

1. Preheat oven to 325°F.

2. Combine the eggs, pumpkin, banana, ground chicken, hot water, and ground ginger in a large bowl. Add the flour and mix until combined.

3. Spoon the batter into a greased mini cupcake pan. Bake for 15 to 18 minutes, until slightly hardened. Allow these to cool completely.

4. Beat the cream cheese with an electric mixer until pale and fluffy. Place it into a piping bag fitted with a #2D star-shaped piping tip. Pipe the cream cheese onto the cupcakes and serve!

5. These treats can be stored in the fridge for up to 5 days or frozen and stored for up to 3 months!

Pup-kin Spice LATTE

It's safe to assume that every pup longingly stares at their owner's pumpkin spice lattes, hoping for a lick. Your dog is amazing and they deserve their very own version!

─────────── MAKES 1 CUP OF LATTE ───────────

½ cup whipping cream
½ cup water
¼ cup plain yogurt
¼ cup plain canned pumpkin

TREACLE TIP: *For an extra festive flavor, add ¼ teaspoon ground ginger to the latte mix!*

1. Beat the whipping cream with an electric mixer until stiff peaks form. Set aside in the fridge.

2. Pour the water, yogurt, and pumpkin into a bowl and whisk together. Pour it into little glasses or bowls.

3. Spoon the whipped cream into a piping bag fitted with a large, star-shaped piping tip. Pipe a dollop on top of each "latte" and serve to your puppies!

Pawsitively Pawfect
DOUGHNUTS

Banana-beef flavor may sound awful to humans, but your doggy will disagree!

3 cups crispy rice cereal
1¼ cups beef or chicken broth
   (page 34)
1¼ cups whole wheat flour
1 cup thinly sliced banana
8 ounces ground beef
1 large egg
Cooking spray
½ cup cream cheese
Grated carrot, for garnish

1. Preheat oven to 350°F.

2. Combine the cereal and broth in a large bowl and soak for 10 minutes. Add the flour, banana, beef, and egg, and mix until well combined.

3. Grease a mini doughnut pan with cooking spray. Spoon the mixture into the pan and bake for 15 minutes. Cool completely.

4. Place the cream cheese in a microwave-safe bowl and microwave for 30-second intervals until melted. Once cooled, dunk the doughnuts into the cream cheese. Grate a carrot over the doughnuts to create sprinkles. Serve to your puppy and enjoy!

5. These doughnuts should be stored in the fridge and eaten within 1 week.

TREACLE TIP: *If your dog has a beef allergy, you can substitute ground chicken or turkey!*

Banana PANCAKES

An adorable weekend treat for your dog! They have been hoping for a bite of your breakfast for years; now you can treat them to a healthy and fun treat. Pictured alongside these pancakes is the Let's Go to Doga Green Smoothie (page 101), a great complement to these hearty pancakes.

— MAKES 10 TO 12 SMALL PANCAKES —

3 large eggs
2 tablespoons liquid coconut oil, plus extra for greasing the pan
2 tablespoons maple syrup
¼ cup coconut flour
1 teaspoon baking powder
10–12 banana slices
Peanut butter, for drizzling

TREACLE TIP: *These pancakes are much softer than human pancakes, so it might take some practice to flip them. A thin spatula and maintaining a small size of pancake are the key to success!*

1. In a large bowl, whisk together the eggs, coconut oil, and maple syrup. Add the coconut flour and baking powder and whisk until just combined.

2. Set a frying pan to medium-low heat. Once the pan is warm, drizzle some coconut oil into the pan. Place tablespoon-sized dollops of pancake batter into the pan. Top each pancake with a banana slice and cook for 3 to 4 minutes, until the bottoms are golden brown.

3. Flip the pancakes and cook for another 3 to 4 minutes.

4. Serve with some peanut butter and a Let's Go to Doga Green Smoothie! These pancakes are best eaten the day they are made, but can be frozen and reheated in the toaster. Just be sure that they aren't too warm when serving to your pup. Bananas can retain quite a lot of heat!

Apple and Oat TRUFFLES

These truffles are packed with fiber, digestion-aiding pumpkin, and healthy fats, which keep your pup's coat beautiful and shiny. Be sure to use unsweetened applesauce, as dogs shouldn't be consuming any excess sugar or sugar substitutes.

—————————————— MAKES ABOUT 18 TO 20 TRUFFLES ——————————————

1 cup whole wheat flour
¼ cup quick cooking oats
2 teaspoons baking powder
¼ cup plain canned pumpkin
¼ cup peanut butter
½ cup unsweetened
    applesauce
¼ cup liquid coconut oil
2 large eggs
1 carrot, grated
8 ounces cream cheese, room
    temperature
1 cup unsalted peanuts, finely
    chopped

1. Preheat the oven to 350°F.

2. In a medium size bowl, combine the flour, oats, and baking powder. Set aside. In a large bowl, combine the pumpkin, peanut butter, applesauce, coconut oil, eggs, and carrot with an electric mixer. Add the dry mixture and mix until just combined.

3. Spoon the batter into a lined cupcake pan. Bake for 15 to 20 minutes, or until a skewer inserted into the center of the cupcakes comes out clean. Cool completely.

4. Remove the liner from the cupcakes and break the cupcakes into a large bowl, then use an electric mixer to further break them into small crumbs. Add the cream cheese and beat with the electric mixer until it is fully incorporated. You should be able to easily mold and shape the mixture.

5. Shape the mixture into balls. Depending on the size of your dog, these can be tablespoon-sized or smaller. I made tablespoon-sized balls and could make about 20.

6. Pour the chopped peanuts into a shallow dish. Press the balls into the peanuts and reshape them into balls, while pressing to thoroughly attach the peanuts.

7. Chill the truffles in the fridge for 1 to 2 hours, until firm.

8. Give to your pup and enjoy! These should be stored in the fridge and should be eaten within 3 to 4 days. They can also be frozen and consumed within 3 months.

Carbonara COOKIES

These cookies were originally intended to be called Bacon and Egg cookies, until I smelled them and realized that they smell exactly like spaghetti carbonara! The doggies were extra lucky this day and were allowed to have a once-in-a-lifetime taste of real spaghetti carbonara during the photo shoot.

———————————— MAKES ABOUT 2 DOZEN (1-INCH) COOKIES ————————————

5 strips bacon, uncooked
1½ cups quick oats
½ cup grated Parmesan cheese
1 tablespoon fresh curly parsley,
　roughly chopped
2 large eggs

1. Preheat oven to 350°F.

2. Cook the bacon in a frying pan set to medium heat. Once the bacon is crispy, place it on a paper towel to absorb any excess oil. Allow the bacon to cool completely, then break into rough pieces.

3. Place the oats in a food processor and pulse until they have ground into a powder. This is a quick way to create a "flour"! Add the Parmesan cheese, parsley, and bacon to the food processor and pulse until all ingredients have been combined and processed together to create a delicious cheesy, meaty flour.

4. Place the mixture in a large bowl and add the eggs. Beat with an electric mixer until thoroughly combined. This dough is a little dense, but quite easy to work with.

5. Roll the dough out between 2 sheets of parchment paper until it is ¼-inch thick. Cut out shapes with a 1-inch cookie cutter.

6. Place the cookies on a baking sheet lined with parchment paper. Bake for 15 to 20 minutes, or until the edges are golden. Cool completely before serving.

Frozen PUMPKIN BONES

These little orange bones are a great treat after autumn walkies. They're also super nutritious! Salmon oil contains omega-3 and omega-6 fatty acids, which are highly beneficial for your dog's skin, fur, immune system, heart, and cognitive function. Pumpkin is rich in fiber, is a rich source of vitamins, and is a digestive aid for pups suffering from constipation or diarrhea. These treats are small, but mighty!

——————————— MAKES ABOUT 40 (1-INCH) BONES ———————————

1 cup Salmon Broth (page 39)
1 cup plain canned pumpkin
½ cup pure salmon oil
1 cup cantaloupe chunks

1. Place all ingredients into a blender or food processor. Blend until the mixture is completely smooth.

2. Pour into a dog bone-shaped silicone mold. Freeze for 3 hours, or until solid.

3. Unmold and feed to your pup!

50 Facts About Treacle

1. She steals Paddington's cookie crumbs, even while he's still eating.

2. She scoots her bum all over the house, even when her bum is clean. (We checked with the vet and groomer, don't worry!)

3. She is a daddy's girl. She loves my boyfriend so much and lets him scratch her belly for hours.

4. She has patches of brown fur around her neck, like a fur collar. #fancy

5. She has a single white hair on her back.

6. One of her whiskers is curly.

7. She is mini size, but her tongue is normal size.

8. She is a laundry princess. No matter if it's clean or dirty laundry, she will roll in it, wiggle, and squeak.

9. After a visitor leaves, she'll look out the window and cry.

10. On cold days, she loves to be tucked into my boyfriend's jacket and peek out the top, like a baby kangaroo.

11. She will hide under the couch and complain when it's time for walkies.

12. She gets very excited when her kibble or water is refilled.

13. When asked if she wants a cookie, she bounces, spins, and barks in pure blissful celebration. Every single time, multiple times a day.

14. She is the perfect purse dog. She happily sits and observes while in a bag.

15. She is an introvert.

16. She'll be completely silent, then let out an insanely loud bark—stops my heart every time.

17. She loves small pieces of cardboard. She'll play and pounce on it for ages.

18. When she is very happy, her tongue will hang out the side of her mouth.

19. She hates being fussed with (brushing, putting her harness on, adjusting outfits).

20. She treats her crate like her bedroom. She brings all her toys and cookies inside for playing or for saving for later. Paddington has learned this and sometimes "breaks in" and has a sniff around.

21. She loves empty toilet paper rolls. She knows the sound of the final square of toilet paper being peeled off the roll and will come running into the bathroom. You can usually find several rolls in her crate.

22. She steals your socks if you take them off and don't put them away.

23. She always sniffs my morning coffee, then looks disgusted and disappointed.

24. She likes to be stroked like a cat.

25. She hides her sassy side from strangers and acts super sweet and gentle. Lies.

26. When eating kibble, she'll carry pieces to her bed and eat them there.

27. She drinks water very daintily.

28. She responds most to the word "Queen."

29. She likes to nibble on her tail.

30. Her fur is so silky and a very different texture from Paddington. It almost never tangles!

31. She is very protective of Paddington if another dog plays too rough with him.

32. If I fall asleep on the couch, she will sleep on the couch cushion next to me.

33. She is like a little mountain goat and climbs all over the couch.

34. She never wants to come back inside after a walk, despite being upset about going on walkies.

35. When on a leash, she'll dig in her heels unless my boyfriend is walking her.

36. She doesn't like walkies.

37. She barks at my boyfriend when he stands in a certain corner of our condo.

38. When she is handed a treat, she starts licking even before I put it in her mouth.

39. Her doggy dad has black fur and her doggy mom has Paddington's fur color.

40. She was the only puppy in her litter.

41. She hates to be brushed.

42. Her name means "molasses" in British English.

43. She will steal tissue or food wrappers if left unattended.

44. She was meant to be named Selene before she became mine.

45. She is quite territorial with cookies.

46. She escorts me to the bathroom every single time.

47. She is sweetest in the mornings, sassiest in the evenings.

48. She loves plastic bottle caps. If you scratch one with your fingernail, it will trigger zoomies.

49. She pulls your hand toward her if you stop petting her and she wants more. If you ignore her the first time, her second pull will be more forceful.

50. If you put her in an empty sink, she will freeze and not move. This has proven to be very useful when I needed to put drops in her ear!

WINTER

Red Velvet CUPCAKES

Red velvet cake is just as popular in the doggy world as it is in the human world, but not without some ingredient changes. Instead of red food dye, we're using beets for the classic red color, and there is no cocoa powder in sight!

───────────── MAKES 3 DOZEN MINI CUPCAKES ─────────────

3 medium-sized beets, peeled and
    quartered
½ cup hot water
2 cups whole wheat flour
½ cup sunflower seed oil
5-ounce can of tuna in water, drained
2 large eggs
2 cups cream cheese, room
    temperature

1. Place the beets in a pot and cover with water. Bring to a boil and cook for 45 minutes, until the beets can be easily pierced with a knife. Drain and place in a food processer and pulse until smooth. This should make about 2 cups of puree. Set aside.

2. Add the hot water, flour, oil, tuna, and eggs and mix until well combined.

3. Dollop into a greased mini muffin tin. Bake at 350°F for 25 minutes until golden brown on top. Cool in the pan for 10 minutes, then transfer the cupcakes to a wire rack and cool completely.

4. Once the cupcakes have fully cooled, beat the cream cheese with an electric mixer until pale and fluffy. Place the cream cheese in a piping bag fitted with a large, star-shaped piping tip. Pipe a dollop of cream cheese onto each cupcake.

5. To store, cover and refrigerate for up to 3 days, or place in a freezer bag and freeze for up to 3 months.

Christmas
CAROB CHIP COOKIES

Carob is a dog-safe alternative to chocolate. It melts in a similar way to chocolate and can be purchased in chip or powder form. In this recipe, we're using carob chips for a cute, safe spin on chocolate chip cookies.

——————————————— MAKES ABOUT 2 DOZEN COOKIES ———————————————

½ cup dried liver treats
2 cups whole wheat flour
1 tablespoon baking powder
½ cup carob chips (*not* chocolate chips)
1 cup natural peanut butter
1–2 cups water

1. Preheat the oven to 375°F.

2. Place the dried liver treats in a food processor and pulse until crumbly. Add the flour, baking powder, and carob chips, and set aside.

3. Combine the peanut butter and 1 cup of water in bowl. Add the dry mixture and mix until well combined. If the mixture is too dry, add a little bit more water. Shape into a ball.

4. Dollop tablespoon-sized balls of dough onto a baking sheet lined with parchment paper.

5. Bake for 20 minutes, until lightly brown. Cool completely and enjoy!

Holiday MILK AND COOKIES

Your fur baby anticipates Santa's arrival just as much as you do! Teach your pup to leave some milk and cookies out and maybe there will be a few extra toys under the tree....

───────── MAKES ABOUT 1 DOZEN LARGE (3-INCH) COOKIES ─────────

4 eggs
1 cup plain canned pumpkin
½ cup coconut oil
½ cup peanut butter
1½ cups organic coconut flour
½ teaspoon baking soda
Baby carrots
Plain yogurt

Make the cookies:

1. Preheat oven to 350°F.

2. Beat the eggs lightly with an electric mixer. Add the pumpkin puree, coconut oil, and peanut butter, and mix until well combined. Add the coconut flour and baking soda and mix until fully incorporated.

3. Shape the dough into 2 balls, wrap in plastic wrap, and chill in the freezer until firm, about 20 minutes.

4. Roll each ball of dough out between 2 sheets of parchment paper. Cut out cookies with cookie cutters, place on a baking sheet lined with parchment paper, and bake for 15 minutes. Cool completely.

To serve:

1. Place mini carrots in a bowl, a dollop of yogurt in a small cup, and the cookies on a tray.

2. Set it out and wait for puppy Santa and reindeer to come!

TREACLE TIP: *Check out the full video on YouTube, where you can see puppy Santa and reindeer arrive!*

Sick Day
CHICKEN & RICE PILAF

This recipe has been recommended to me by my vet multiple times for use when the pups have an upset tummy and need a bland diet for a few days. Hopefully your dog isn't as sassy as Paddington and doesn't pick out the chicken and leave the rice. Seriously, Paddington?

——————————————— MAKES ROUGHLY 2½ CUPS ———————————————

2 cups chicken broth (page 37)
½ cup uncooked brown rice
1 raw chicken breast

1. Place the chicken broth and rice in a large pot and set to high heat. Once it comes to a boil, add the chicken breast. Boil for 15 minutes, or until both the rice and chicken breast are fully cooked.

2. Drain the excess broth. Shred the chicken breast and mix with the rice.

3. Serve to your puppy.

> **TREACLE TIP:** *This is also a great emergency meal if you are caught without dog food and your pup needs to eat. Be sure to consult with your vet regarding how much of this your dog should consume as a meal replacement.*

Peanut Butter and Beet
STARS

These are delicious, soft, cakey cookies. I initially made these for Paddington to celebrate Lunar New Year because of their vibrant red color.

—————————————— MAKES ABOUT 60 (¾-INCH) COOKIES ——————————————

1 large beet, boiled, peeled, and pureed
2 large eggs
½ cup natural peanut butter
2½ cups whole wheat flour

1. Preheat oven to 350°F.

2. Combine the beet, eggs, and peanut butter in a large bowl. Add the flour and mix to combine. If the mixture is slightly dry, add up to ¼ cup water.

3. Roll the dough out on a floured surface to ¼-inch thick. Cut into shapes with your desired cookie cutter.

4. Place on a baking sheet lined with parchment paper and bake for 10 to 15 minutes.

5. Cool completely and enjoy!

TREACLE TIP: *Be sure not to use canned beets, as they can sometimes contain additives that are harmful to dogs. Fresh beets are the best route to go!*

Spirulina CHRISTMAS COOKIES

Spirulina contains several phytonutrients that strengthen the immune system, improve gastrointestinal health, and help allergies. It is also incredibly helpful for the holidays, since it turns cookies a festive green!

───────────── MAKES 40 (1-INCH) TREATS ─────────────

1 teaspoon spirulina
1¼ cups brown rice flour
¼ cup liquid coconut oil
⅔ cup chicken broth
Red sugar sprinkles

1. Preheat oven to 325°F.

2. Combine all ingredients in a bowl. The dough should resemble playdough. If it's too dry, add an extra 1 to 2 tablespoons of chicken broth.

3. Fill a cookie press with the cookie dough.

4. Line a baking sheet with parchment paper and press the cookies onto the baking sheet. Sprinkle red sugar sprinkles onto the cookies.

5. Bake for 15 to 20 minutes, until the edges are just starting to brown.

6. Cool completely and then give to your pup!

Homestyle PUPPY STEW

This recipe was given to me from Paddington and Treacle's breeder when I first brought them home. We use this recipe after they have surgical procedures, or if they're in need of some comfort food. They have become so familiar with the food that they recognize the smell when I'm cooking!

——————————— MAKES ABOUT 6 CUPS OF STEW ———————————

2 cups brown rice
2 sweet potatoes
4 large carrots
1 tablespoon olive oil
2 sticks celery
2 pounds ground beef
Fresh parsley (optional)

TREACLE TIP: *Freeze in small portions to make easy, ready-to-go meals. Divide the stew into zip-top bags, and store them all in one larger Ziploc bag to prevent freezer burn. To defrost, simply place one portion in the fridge overnight and it will be ready to eat the next day!*

1. Cook the rice according to the package instructions. Set aside.

2. Peel the sweet potatoes and carrots and cut into large chunks. Place into a pot and cover with water. Bring the water to a boil and cook until both the potatoes and carrots can be easily pierced with a knife, about 10 to 15 minutes. Drain, then roughly mash together with a fork or potato masher. Some lumps are fine, depending on your dog's preference. Set aside.

3. Set a large frying pan to medium heat and add the olive oil. Dice the celery and add it to the pan. Cook until soft. Add the ground beef and cook until browned and cooked through.

4. Add the mashed sweet potato and carrot mixture, as well as the rice, and mix until everything is fully combined.

5. Remove the pan from the heat and cool completely. For an extra special touch, serve with a fresh sprig of parsley—hopefully your dog will enjoy it and not spit it out, like Treacle did.

ADVENT CALENDAR
for Dogs

Advent calendars are arguably one of the best parts of the holidays, so your pup should be in on the fun too! If your dog is big enough to knock your Christmas tree over, I suggest hanging the calendar on a higher, sturdier surface. No toppling over Christmas trees this season!

— MAKES 24 COOKIES —

1 large egg
1 cup quick-cooking oats
½ cup shredded part-skim mozzarella cheese
½ cup organic peanut butter
⅛ cup hot water
24 small burlap pouches
Markers or paint
Mini clothespins
Festive ribbon

1. Preheat oven to 325°F.

2. Beat the egg in a large bowl. Add the oats, cheese, peanut butter, and water and mix well.

3. Divide into 24 pieces and shape into cookies.

4. Place on a baking sheet lined with parchment paper and bake for 15 to 18 minutes, until slightly hardened. Cool the cookies completely.

5. Label 24 mini pouches 1 through 24 with some markers or paint. Place a cookie inside of each envelope, then attach the envelopes to a string and hang in your desired location.

TREACLE TIP: *These cookies stay fresh at room temperature for 3 days, so I recommend placing the cookies in a freezer bag, freezing them, and defrosting 3 at a time at room temperature overnight. Your pup won't know they haven't been in their individual pouches the whole time, and they'll be getting wholesome, fresh treats each morning!*

Gimme Some More
MEATLOAF

Turkey is a great source of nutrients and protein, and a homemade meatloaf is a fun way to treat your dog! This meatloaf has hard boiled eggs in it, giving it an extra wow factor when sliced! Your pup might not appreciate the visual, but they will surely enjoy the taste.

—————————— MAKES 1 (8X4-INCH) MEATLOAF ——————————

1 pound lean ground turkey
1 large egg, lightly beaten
⅓ cup quick oats
⅓ cup frozen cranberries, thawed
½ cup diced carrots
½ cup diced green beans (fresh or frozen)
½ cup cooked brown rice
¼ cup grated Parmesan cheese
4 hard-boiled eggs
Coconut oil, for pan

1. Preheat oven to 375°F.

2. Combine all ingredients, except for the hard-boiled eggs and coconut oil, in a large bowl.

3. Grease a 5x7-inch loaf pan with coconut oil. Pour half of the meatloaf mix into the pan. Place the hard-boiled eggs on top, then cover with the remaining meatloaf mix.

4. Bake for 45 minutes. Cool completely, then slice up for your pup! This can be stored in the fridge for 2 to 3 days, or frozen for up to 3 months.

TREACLE TIP: *Freeze this meatloaf in individual slices, so that you can defrost it a slice at a time! More meatloaf snackies is never a problem in my book.*

Star of David
COCONUT COOKIES

Happy Hanukkah from the puppies! These sweet treats contain coconut, which is great for your dog's skin and fur. We're using blue spirulina to dye the cookies blue and get you in the Hanukkah spirit!

——————————————— MAKES 40 (1-INCH) TREATS ———————————————

1¼ cups brown rice flour
¼ cup liquid coconut oil
⅔ cup chicken broth
1 teaspoon blue spirulina
¼ cup unsweetened coconut flakes

1. Preheat oven to 325°F.

2. Combine all ingredients in a bowl. The dough should resemble play dough. If it's too dry, add an extra 1 to 2 tablespoons of chicken broth.

3. Roll the dough out on a floured surface until it is ¼-inch-thick. Use a 1-inch Star of David cookie cutter to cut out shapes. Transfer them to a baking sheet lined with parchment paper.

4. Bake the cookies for 15 minutes, until they are hard and just beginning to brown at the edges.

5. Cool completely and serve to your doggy! These cookies should be stored in the fridge and consumed within 1 week.

Steak & Sweet Potato STEW

Sometimes your dog deserves to eat a gourmet meal. This is the meal for those times. I genuinely felt like I was cooking for myself with all the braising and sautéing, but it was so worth it to see the excitement in Paddington's and Treacle's eyes. The look of awe when Treacle picked up a cube of meat and tasted its vibrant, beefy juices was precious.

———————————— MAKES ABOUT 8 CUPS OF STEW ————————————

3 pounds beef chuck (or steak, if your doggy is feeling extra fancy)

3 tablespoons coconut oil

2 celery stalks, thinly sliced

2 apples, peeled, cored, and cut into ½-inch chunks

¼ cup rice flour

6 cups beef broth

3 tablespoons fresh curly parsley, finely chopped, plus extra for garnish

1 cup brown rice, uncooked

4 carrots, cut into 1-inch chunks

1 pound sweet potatoes, peeled and sliced into 1-inch cubes

½ cup frozen peas

TREACLE TIP: *Save some for me if you make this for your pup!*

1. Preheat the oven to 325°F.

2. Pat the meat dry with a paper towel, then cut into 1½-inch pieces. If your dog is on the smaller side, you can cut it into smaller pieces.

3. Set a heavy soup pot to medium high heat and add the coconut oil. Add the steak in 2 to 3 batches, browning the chunks on all sides. Transfer the steak to a plate and set aside.

4. Add the celery and apples to the pot and cook for 5 minutes, until soft. The celery and apple will absorb the residual steak flavors and will make your pup very happy!

5. Return the steak to the pan and add the rice flour. Stir until the flour has dissolved, about 2 minutes.

6. Add the beef broth and parsley. Mix well. Bring the pot to a boil, then cover with a lid and place the pot into the oven.

7. Braise the meat for 2 hours. Then remove from the oven and add the rice, carrots, sweet potatoes, and frozen peas. Cover the pot and return it to the oven and cook for 1 additional hour.

8. Allow the stew to cool completely, then garnish with some more parsley and feed to your dog!

Valentine's Day
HEART COOKIES

Who is more deserving of Valentine's Day cookies than your puppy, who loves you unconditionally? These cookies are naturally pink, making them even more adorable!

—————————————— MAKES 60 (2-INCH) COOKIES ——————————————

¾ cup frozen cranberries, thawed
¾ cup frozen strawberries, thawed
2 eggs
½ cup peanut butter
½ cup chicken broth
3–3½ cups brown rice flour
¼ cup carob chips
1 teaspoon liquid coconut oil

TREACLE TIP: *Cranberries are very tart and can be a shock to dogs, but their flavor becomes much more mild in these cookies. Even if your pup has turned up their nose to cranberries in the past, give these cookies a try!*

1. Preheat the oven to 350°F and line a baking sheet with parchment paper.

2. Blend all berries together in a food processor and measure out 1 cup of puree.

3. Add to a bowl with the eggs, peanut butter, and broth. Gradually add the flour until you achieve a smooth, soft dough (you may not need all the flour).

4. Between 2 sheets of floured parchment paper, roll out the dough to ¼-inch thick. Gently remove the top sheet and cut out cookies with a small, heart-shaped cookie cutter, placing them on your prepared baking sheet. Bake for 10 to 15 minutes, until just starting to brown. Allow to cool completely.

5. Microwave the carob chips in a bowl at 30-second intervals, stirring, until melted. Add coconut oil and mix well. Place into a piping bag fitted with a small, round piping tip. Pipe drizzles or messages onto the cookies, then let harden for about 30 minutes.

6. Store the cookies in the fridge for up to 1 week.

Glamour Pup FROSTED RUBIES

Beets are one of my favorite ingredients for dog treats because of their beautiful color! Beets can also stain, but I've got you covered for this recipe! With the help of gelatin, the rubies will maintain their shape (and juice) even at room temperature, so fears of a beet-stained kitchen will be a thing of the past!

——————————— MAKES ROUGHLY 2 CUPS OF TREATS ———————————

1 small beet, boiled and peeled
1¼ cups water, divided
¼ cup plain yogurt
2½ tablespoons gelatin

1. Place the beet, 1 cup water, and yogurt in a blender or food processor and pulse until smooth. Set aside.

2. In a microwave safe bowl, combine the gelatin and ¼ cup water. Allow the gelatin to develop for 5 minutes. Microwave for 20 to 30 seconds, until the gelatin has melted. Add this to the beet mixture and mix well.

3. Pour the mixture into gem-shaped silicone molds and transfer them to the freezer. Chill for 2 to 3 hours, until the rubies are frozen solid.

4. Simply unmold and give to your pup!

TREACLE TIP: *Beets maintain their pretty color all throughout dogs' enjoyment of them, so don't be alarmed to see reddish stool. But always contact your vet if you feel concerned.*

Gingerbread DOGGIES

Ginger is a fantastic ingredient for dog treats! It can help reduce nausea in dogs, which can be a helpful tool with all the traveling we do during the holidays. Give them a cookie before or during a car ride to soothe their tummy and hopefully avoid carsickness.

———————— MAKES 15 TO 20 COOKIES ————————

3 tablespoons olive oil
¼ cup + 2 tablespoons water
¼ cup molasses
1 teaspoon freshly grated ginger
2 teaspoons ground ginger
1½ cups all-purpose flour

1. Combine the olive oil, water, molasses, and fresh ginger with an electric mixer. Add the ground ginger and flour and mix until just combined.

2. Wrap the dough in plastic wrap and chill in the fridge for 1 hour.

3. Preheat the oven to 325°F. Roll the dough out between 2 sheets of plastic wrap. Cut out cookies and place them on a baking sheet lined with parchment paper.

4. Bake the cookies for 20 minutes. Cool completely, then give to your pup!

TREACLE TIP: *Are your puppies jumping all over you when trying to wrap presents? These festive cookies will get them in the holiday spirit, but also keep them away from the wrapping paper!*

Nana's RISOTTO

When my pups visit their nana's house, they sometimes get spoiled with this delicious risotto.
They only eat about ¼ cup at a time, as it is quite heavy and filling.

———————————— MAKES ABOUT 3 CUPS OF RISOTTO ————————————

1 tablespoon coconut oil
1 sweet potato, baked
1 cup Arborio rice
3 cups homemade broth (page 34)

1. Set a pan to medium high heat and add the coconut oil. Scrape out the cooked sweet potato into the pan (we don't use the skin here). Once the sweet potato begins to sizzle, add the rice and stir to combine.

2. Reduce the heat to medium. Add the stock ¼ cup at a time, while continuously stirring. When the stock has evaporated, add another ¼ cup stock. Continue adding stock until the rice is soft, but not mushy.

3. Allow the risotto to cool until it is just warm. Give it a stir, as it can get stiff as it cools, then serve to your pup!

Christmas DINNER

My dogs are quite small, so I've treated them to a mini holiday dinner! This dinner is packed with highly nutritious goodies, which will leave your pup feeling full and satisfied. If you have a larger dog, the Cornish hen can be substituted with a chicken, just be sure to adjust the cooking time accordingly.

———— MAKES 1 CORNISH HEN, 1½ CUPS STUFFING, 2 CUPS SAUTÉED GREEN BEANS ————

Stuffing
3 strips uncooked bacon
½ sweet potato, finely diced
¼ cup frozen cranberries, thawed
2 tablespoons whole flax seeds

Main Dish
1 Cornish hen
String for trussing
1 large sweet potato
2 tablespoons coconut oil, divided
⅔ cup chicken broth

Green Beans
1 tablespoon coconut oil
2 cups fresh green beans, cut into
   bite-sized pieces

TREACLE TIP: *Placing sweet potatoes underneath the Cornish hen is a trick that even humans can try with roasted chicken! The delicious drippings from the chicken makes the sweet potatoes taste absolutely incredible.*

Make the stuffing:
1. Set a frying pan to medium-high heat. Add the bacon and cook until crispy. Set the bacon on a plate lined with paper towel to absorb extra grease. Dispose of most of the grease in the pan, leaving only a tablespoon or so in the pan. Once the bacon has cooled, break it into small pieces.

2. Place the finely diced sweet potato in the pan and cook over medium heat until it is fully cooked and the edges are browned, about 5 to 10 minutes. Then add the cranberries, flax seeds, and bacon back in. Cook until the cranberries have blistered, about 3 minutes.

3. Transfer the stuffing to a bowl and cool completely.

Prepare the Cornish hen:
1. Rinse the Cornish hen with water and check the cavity for any innards or the neck, and discard these if present. Preheat the oven to 450°F.

(Continued)

2. Stuff the cavity with the stuffing. Set aside any leftover stuffing, as it can be enjoyed on its own as well.

3. Tie the "ankles" of the Cornish hen together with string, also known as trussing. This will keep the legs close to the body and prevent them from overcooking while in the oven.

4. Chop the sweet potato into 1-inch cubes. Place these into a baking dish and drizzle with 1 tablespoon coconut oil. Toss to coat.

5. Place the Cornish hen directly on top of the sweet potatoes. Brush the remaining tablespoon of coconut oil onto the entire surface of the hen. This will make it brown beautifully!

6. Roast the Cornish hen for 25 minutes. Then reduce the heat to 350°F. Pour the chicken broth over the hen. Continue roasting for 25 more minutes, basting the hen with the pan juices every 10 minutes. If the hen is browning too much, gently tent the hen with aluminum foil.

7. The hen will be finished cooking when it is golden brown and the juices run clear. Allow the hen to cool before serving it to your dog.

Cook the green beans:
1. While the hen is roasting, cook the green beans. In the same pan that you cooked the stuffing, add the coconut oil and set it to medium heat.

2. Cook the beans until they are vibrant green, about 3 to 4 minutes. At this point they will be tender, but still have some bite to them.

To serve:
1. Remove the skin from the hen and be sure to not serve your dogs any bones. Poultry bones, especially when cooked, are very easy to splinter and can cause blockages and even puncture the stomach or intestine. The meaty flesh is the best part!

2. Add some stuffing, green beans, and roasted sweet potatoes to their plate. Wish them happy holidays and watch them enjoy their mini feast!

Naughty Puppies

Although he might look like a little angel, Paddington can be quite naughty! Here arc some fun stories of his crazy shenanigans.

Chicken Only

When Paddington had an upset tummy and had to go on a bland food diet, I made him some chicken and rice. He clearly wasn't feeling too sick because he picked out all the chicken and left the rice all over the floor! If you're interested in the recipe, check out Sick Day Chicken & Rice Pilaf on page 183!

Stressful Bears

One afternoon, Paddington came running into my bedroom trying to get my attention. I followed him out into the living room and discovered that he had torn open my bag of candy cane gummy bears and scattered them all. over. the. room. Eating a potentially huge quantity of candy is terrifying in itself, but these were peppermint flavor and I wasn't sure if they contained xylitol, which is a very toxic artificial sweetener for dogs and has a slight mint taste. With tears in my eyes, I picked Paddington up and ran him all the way to the vet. Luckily our vet is only a 20-minute walk away, but let me tell you, that was the longest run of my life. We got him to the doctor, pumped his tummy, and called the gummy manufacturer to ask for a list of ingredients. In an incredibly lucky twist of fate, there wasn't any xylitol in the gummies and there weren't any gummy bears in his tummy at all! Was he just trying to show me the mess he made? I've never left any food in reach of the pups since and thankfully haven't had any more food scares.

Studio Invasion

I used to use a separate room to film my recipes. With daily shoots, the floor could get quite dirty and sprinkled in crumbs. Paddington knew that he wasn't allowed inside and always sat right in the doorway as I filmed. One day I must have not shut the studio door completely. I walked by to see two little feet sticking out from under my worktable and heard the sound of licking. I had to pull Paddington out from underneath the table, covered in sprinkles from that day's shoot and very unhappy that I discovered him.

The Glorious Kebab

One evening I made the mistake of leaving a garbage bag in my hallway unattended for an hour or so. Based on Paddington's track record with food, you'd think I would've known this would be a target, but alas, I was naïve. An odd silence came across my condo—a dangerous silence. A silence that is too quiet for an innocent doggy. I walked down the hallway to see Paddington munching and pulling on the garbage bag, that now had a huge hole in the side of it! He heard me gasp, quickly grabbed what he was chewing on, and did a very silly waddle down the hallway. Much to his displeasure, I caught up to him and discovered that he had found a leftover lamb kebab from my dinner the night before! That was the end of the kebab for poor Paddington, but not the end of his garbage bag obsession. I'm sure there will be more stories to come!

The Butter Incident

By now, I'm sure you can tell that almost every story about Paddington deals with food. This is because his daily life involves trying to steal food at every possible moment. In this moment, I learned not to leave groceries on the floor unattended. I heard some rustling, so I walked down the hallway to see that Paddington had torn into a whole brick of butter and had eaten about ⅓ cup! He ran under the couch and was not feeling very well. I called the emergency vet and learned that he was at risk of pancreatitis because of the large quantity of butter. Thankfully he turned out fine—he threw up a couple of times and was back to himself the next day. This actually led to the earlier story, "Chicken Only." The naughtiness never ends with this one.

Lying for a Cookie

Because we live in a condo, I purchased a Porch Potty, which is a fantastic faux grass patch with drainage that I keep on my balcony. Paddington has learned that he gets a cookie every time he goes to the bathroom. One day he did his little routine of jumping on the porch potty, squatting while doing his signature "potty face," then trotting over to me for a cookie. But something felt off. I bent down and felt his tummy and lo and behold, he was completely dry! When I called him out, he got very playful and he knew he got caught! I'm now always on the lookout for this sneaky little trick and I've caught him multiple times since.

The Mortadella Thief

For me and my boyfriend's anniversary, we set out a picnic on our terrace complete with Italian meats, cheeses, and Aperol spritz, and brought out the dogs for a beautiful afternoon. We turned our back to Paddington for half a second and turned back around to see an entire slice of mortadella disappear into his mouth. What I wouldn't give to hear his thoughts as he approached the mortadella and ate it with success. The most heartbreaking part of the story? We only had two slices of mortadella, so my boyfriend and I had to share the remaining piece.

ACKNOWLEDGMENTS

First, I have to thank my puppies, Paddington and Treacle. I knew that Paddington was meant to come into my life years before I'd even met him. He and Treacle have brought so much love and joy into my life; not a day goes by without laughter, cuddles, and kisses. They are my babies and I feel so lucky to spoil them and be their dog mama.

Secondly, I'd like to thank my incredible editor at Skyhorse Publishing, Leah Zarra. Thank you for being so incredibly supportive, helpful, and excited about this book. I have been dreaming of writing a dog cookbook for years and it's because of you that this dream has come true. It's always such a pleasure to work with you and I really hope that we can continue working together long into the future.

I'd also like to thank my lovely boyfriend, Marco. He was in the MVP behind all the photos in this book, whether it was restraining Paddington from running onto the set and eating all the food before it was photographed, or coaching and guiding the pups on where to sit, look, and nibble. I genuinely couldn't have done it

without his help, particularly with the cover photo when Paddington decided that looking away was much more fun than looking at the camera. Thank you my lovey, you are the best daddy to the dogs and best partner I could ever ask for.

Another wonderful human who deserves a thank you is my graphic designer! The adorable graphics you've seen throughout this book have been made by Leyla from CockatooDesign (@cockatoo_design on Instagram). She creates many of the designs you may have seen on my merchandise and created so many custom graphics for this cookbook. Leyla, you are a dream to work with and your work has made this book so beautiful and vibrant!

Last, but absolutely never least, is all of *you*! Without the support, enthusiasm, likes, follows, and comments from my readers, I would not be here. It's as simple as that. Thank you from the bottom of my heart for the time you have taken to enjoy my content. I feel like the luckiest girl in the world to be able to write a cookbook about my dogs and stick photos of them everywhere inside of it. You make me want to work harder and better every day. I am so touched so see photos of your dogs enjoying my dog treat recipes. I hope you know just how much I appreciate you and the incredible gift that each and every one of you have given me.

CONVERSION CHARTS

Metric and Imperial Conversions

(These conversions are rounded for convenience)

Ingredient	Cups/Tablespoons/Teaspoons	Ounces	Grams/Milliliters
Butter	1 cup/ 16 tablespoons/ 2 sticks	8 ounces	230 grams
Cheese, shredded	1 cup	4 ounces	110 grams
Cream cheese	1 tablespoon	0.5 ounce	14.5 grams
Cornstarch	1 tablespoon	0.3 ounce	8 grams
Flour, all-purpose	1 cup/1 tablespoon	4.5 ounces/0.3 ounce	125 grams/8 grams
Flour, whole wheat	1 cup	4 ounces	120 grams
Fruit, dried	1 cup	4 ounces	120 grams
Fruits or veggies, chopped	1 cup	5 to 7 ounces	145 to 200 grams
Fruits or veggies, pureed	1 cup	8.5 ounces	245 grams
Honey, maple syrup, or corn syrup	1 tablespoon	0.75 ounce	20 grams
Liquids: cream, milk, water, or juice	1 cup	8 fluid ounces	240 milliliters
Oats	1 cup	5.5 ounces	150 grams
Spices: cinnamon, cloves, ginger, or nutmeg (ground)	1 teaspoon	0.2 ounce	5 milliliters

Oven Temperatures

Fahrenheit	Celsius	Gas Mark
225°	110°	¼
250°	120°	½
275°	140°	1
300°	150°	2
325°	160°	3
350°	180°	4
375°	190°	5
400°	200°	6
425°	220°	7
450°	230°	8

INDEX